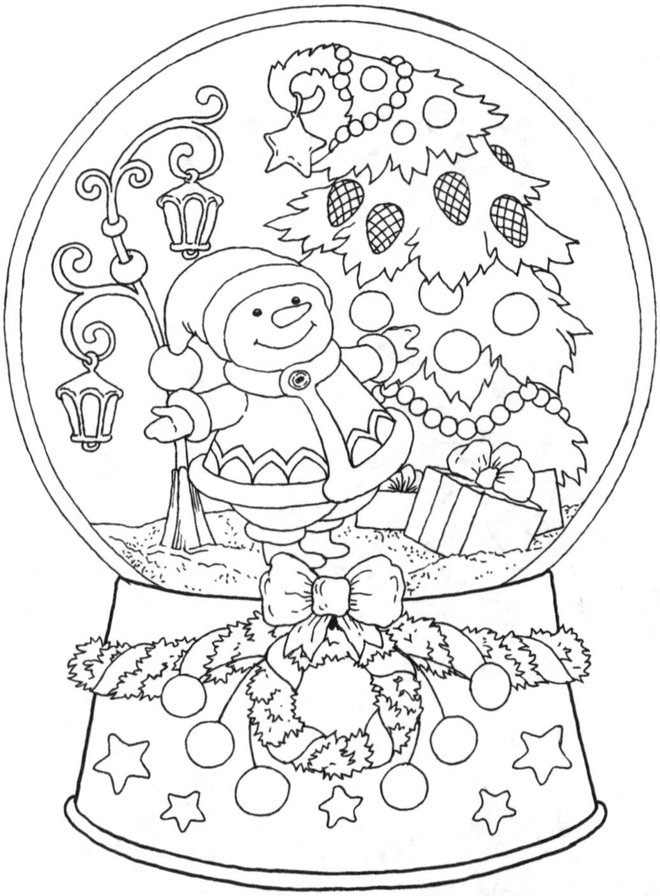

THIS BOOK BELONGS TO

Trustant RACK

NICE LITTLE TOWN
INTERIORS

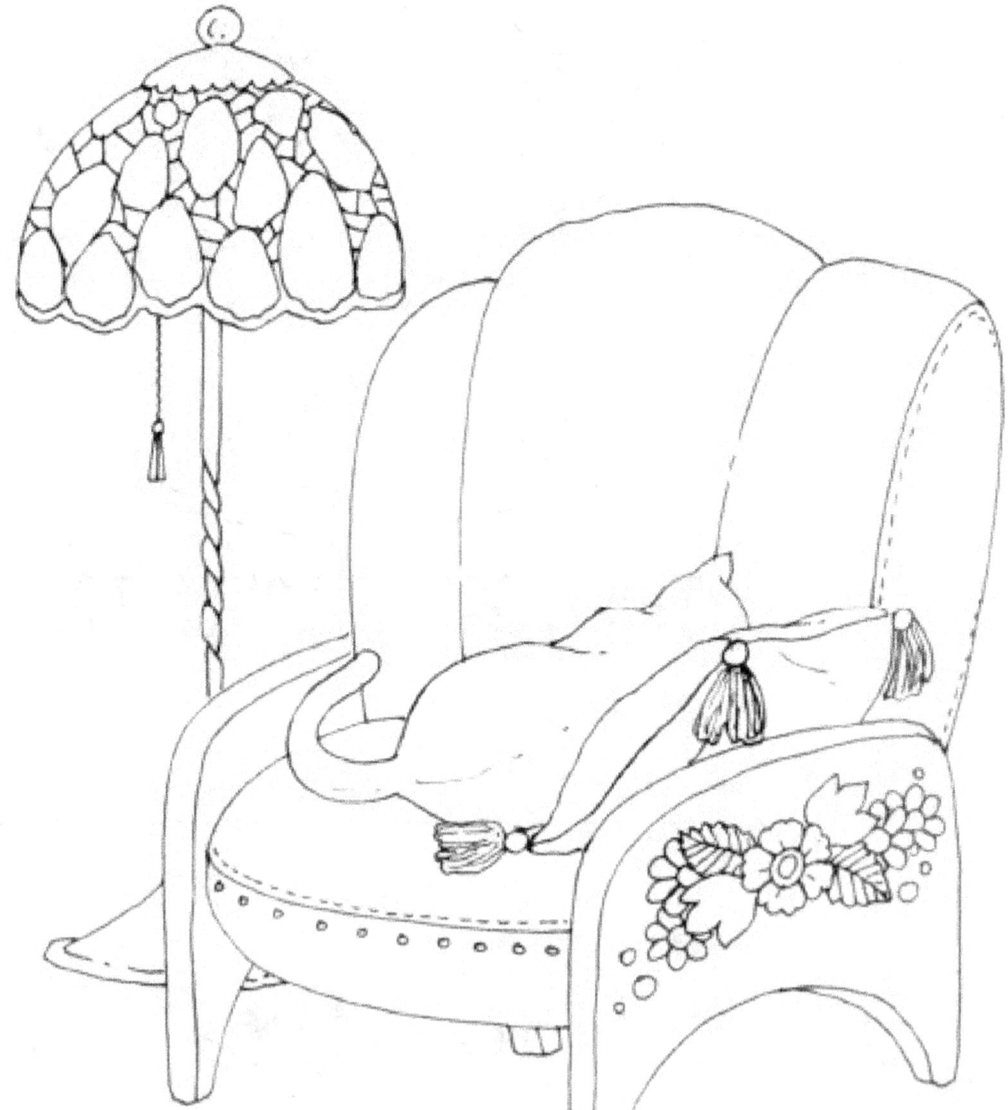

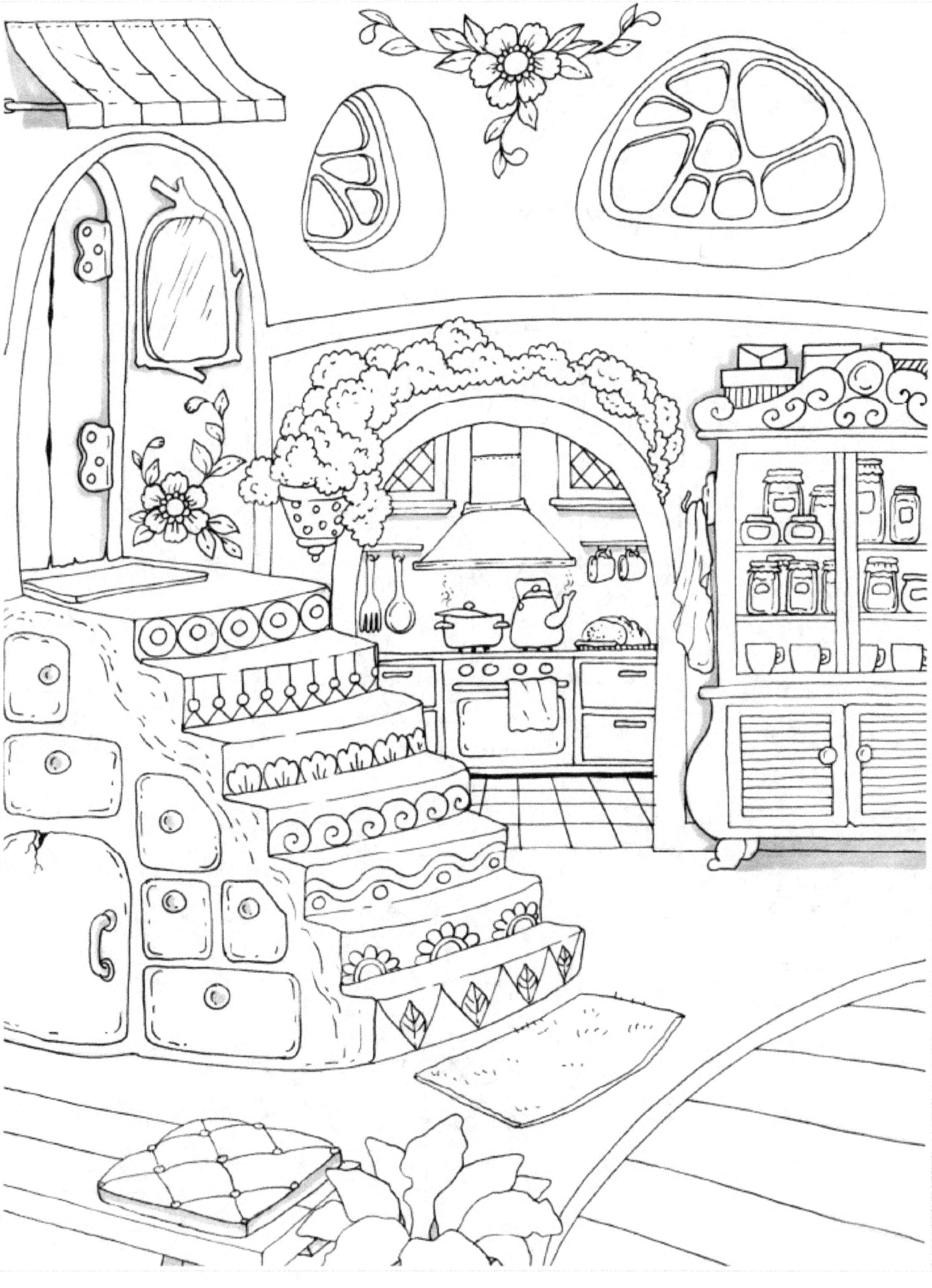

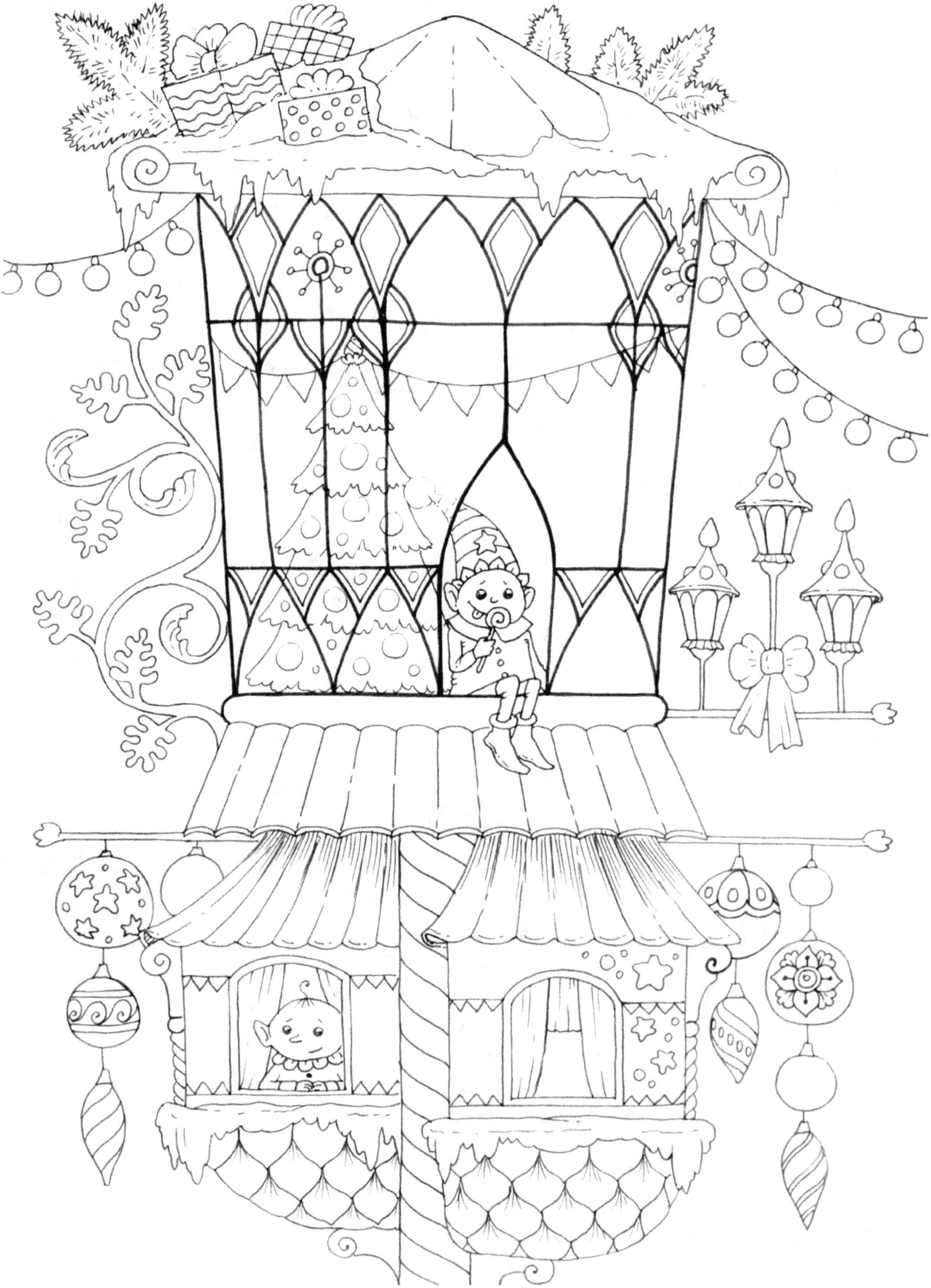

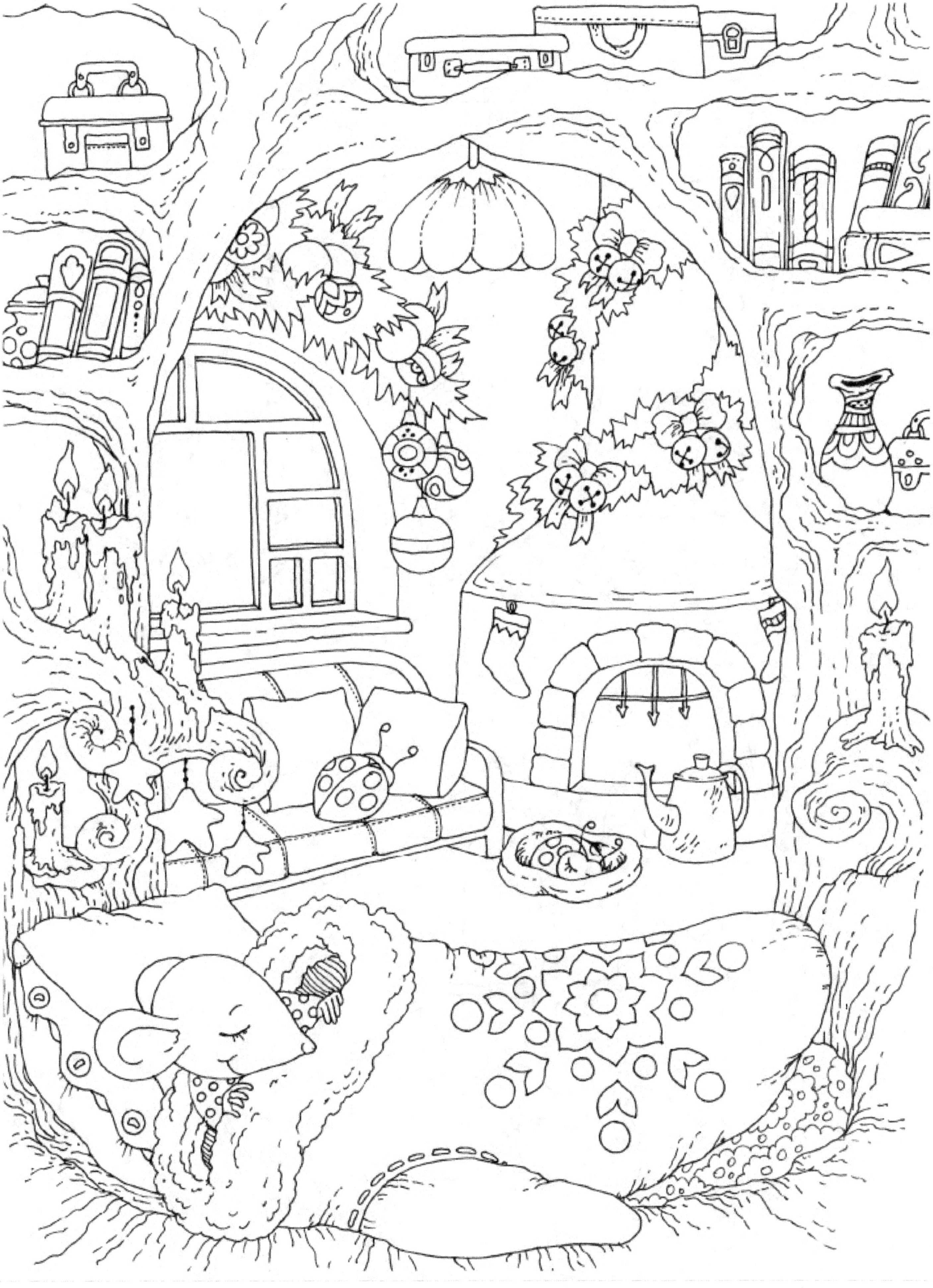

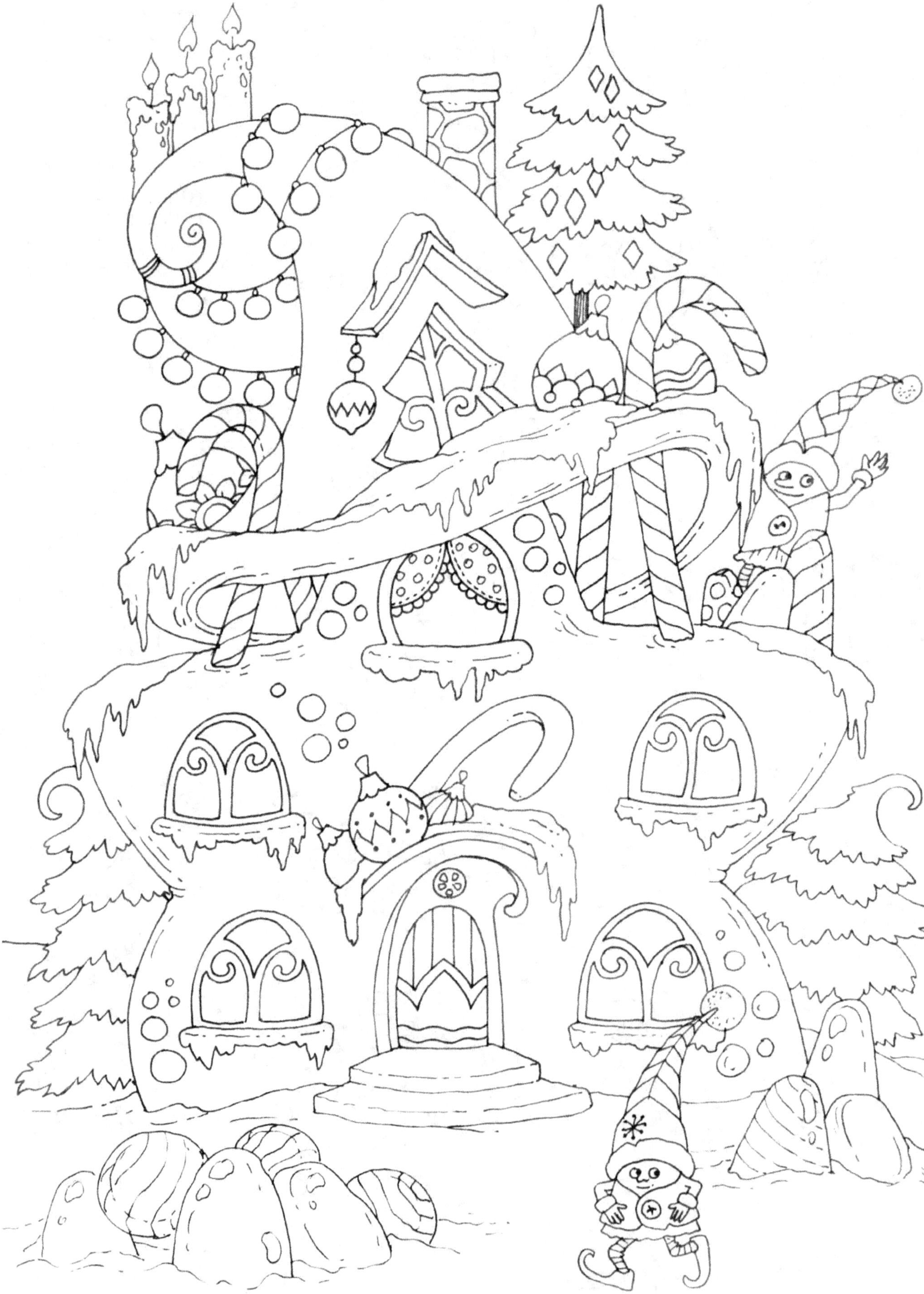

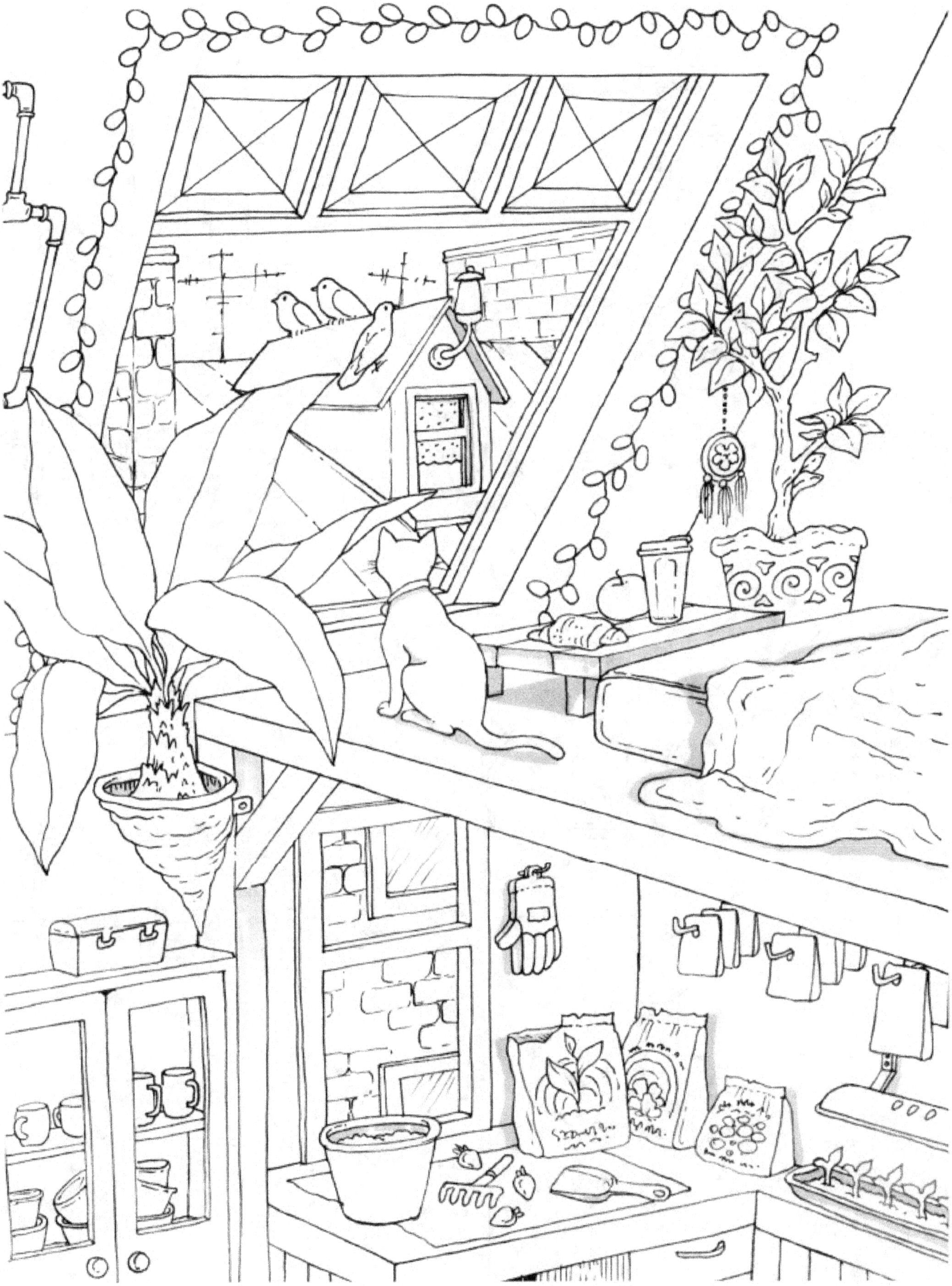

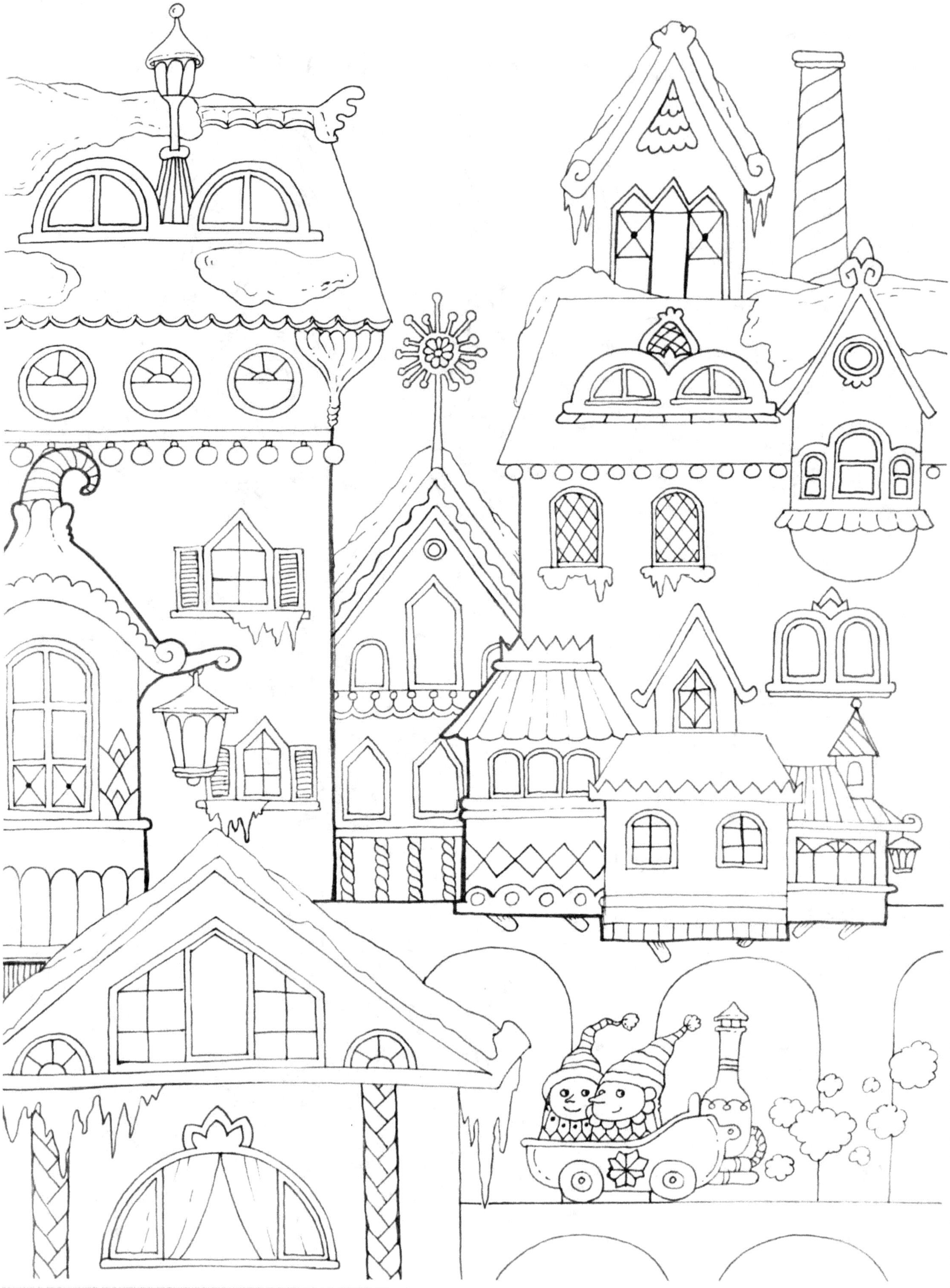

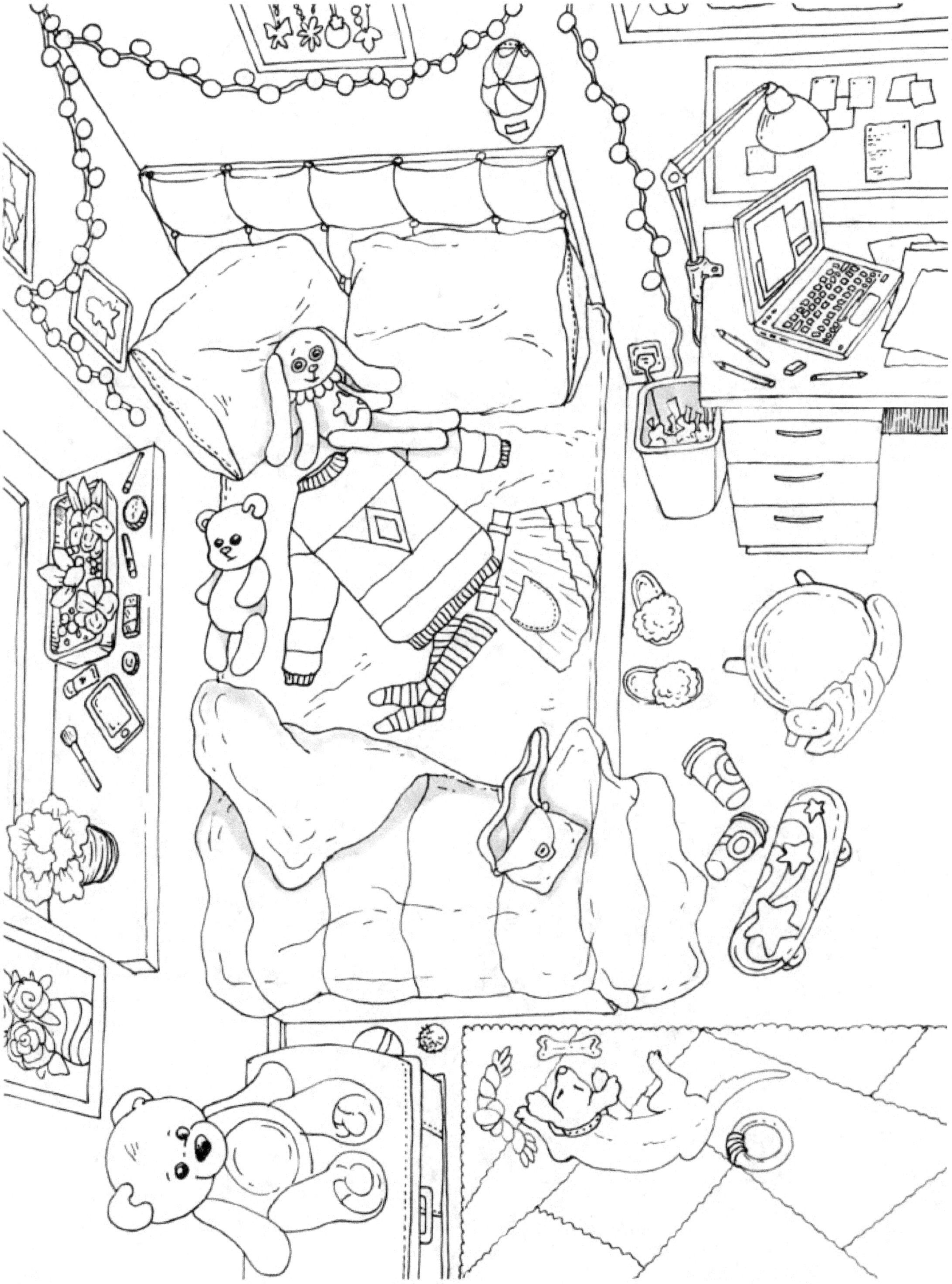

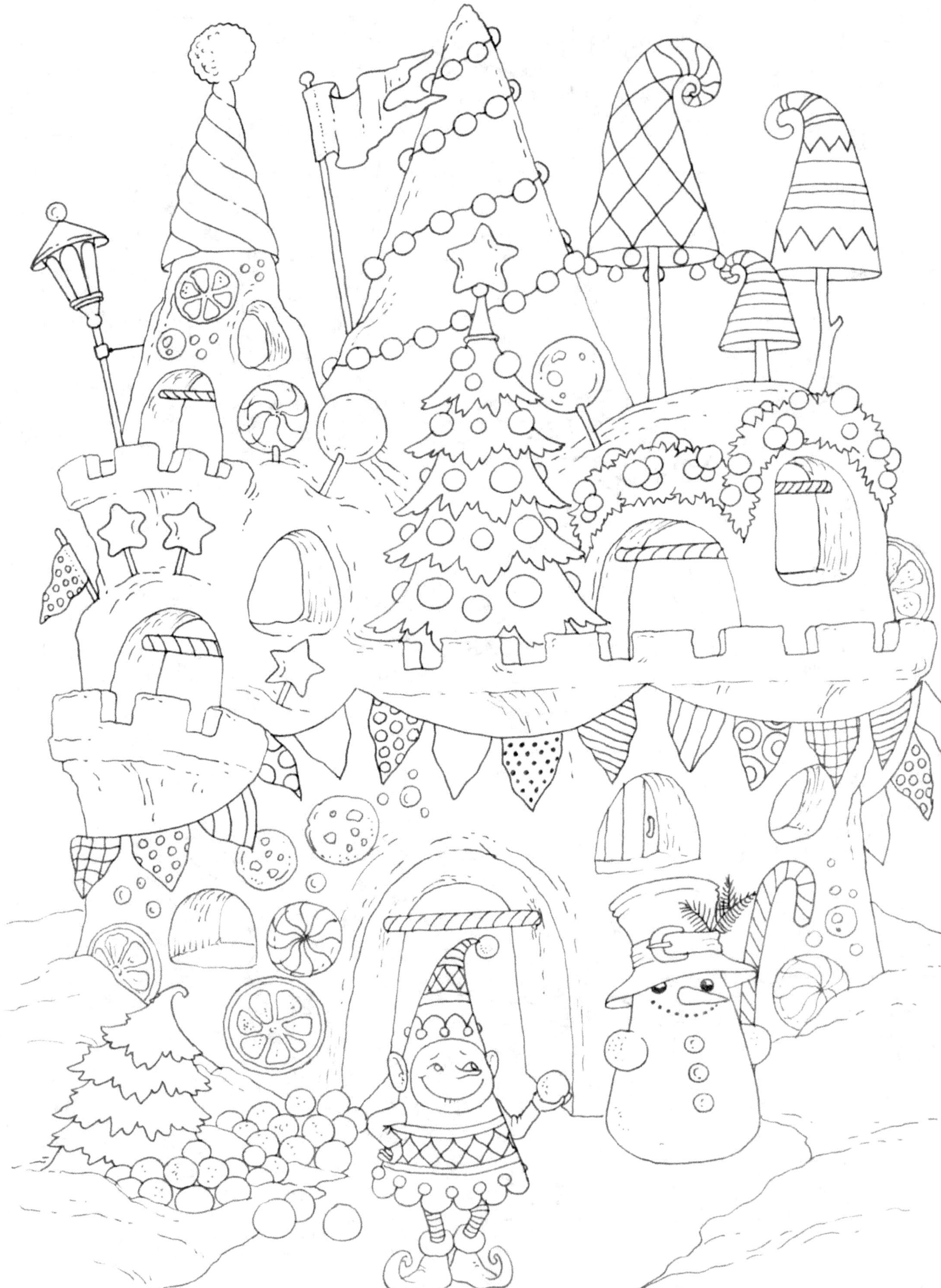

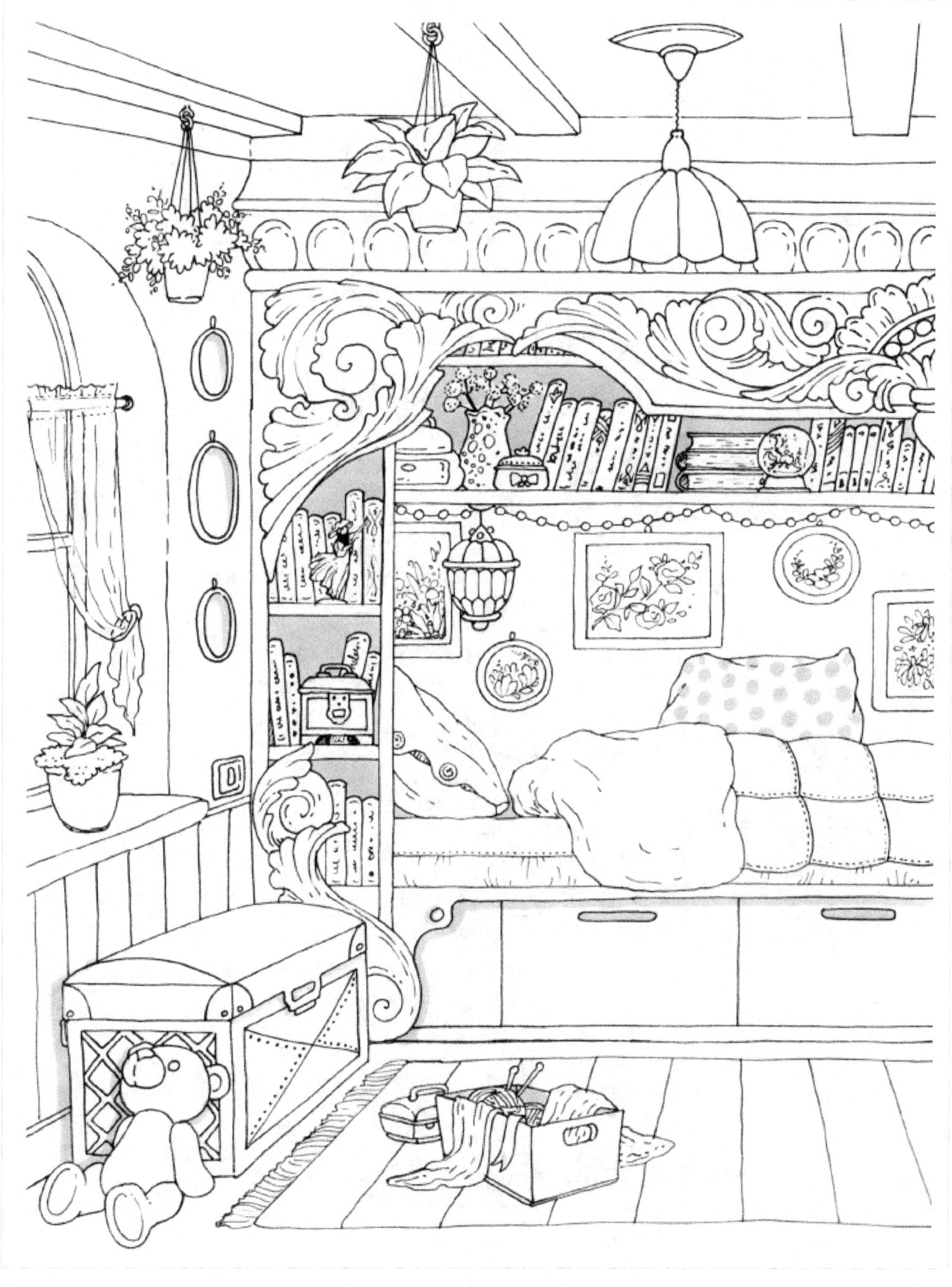

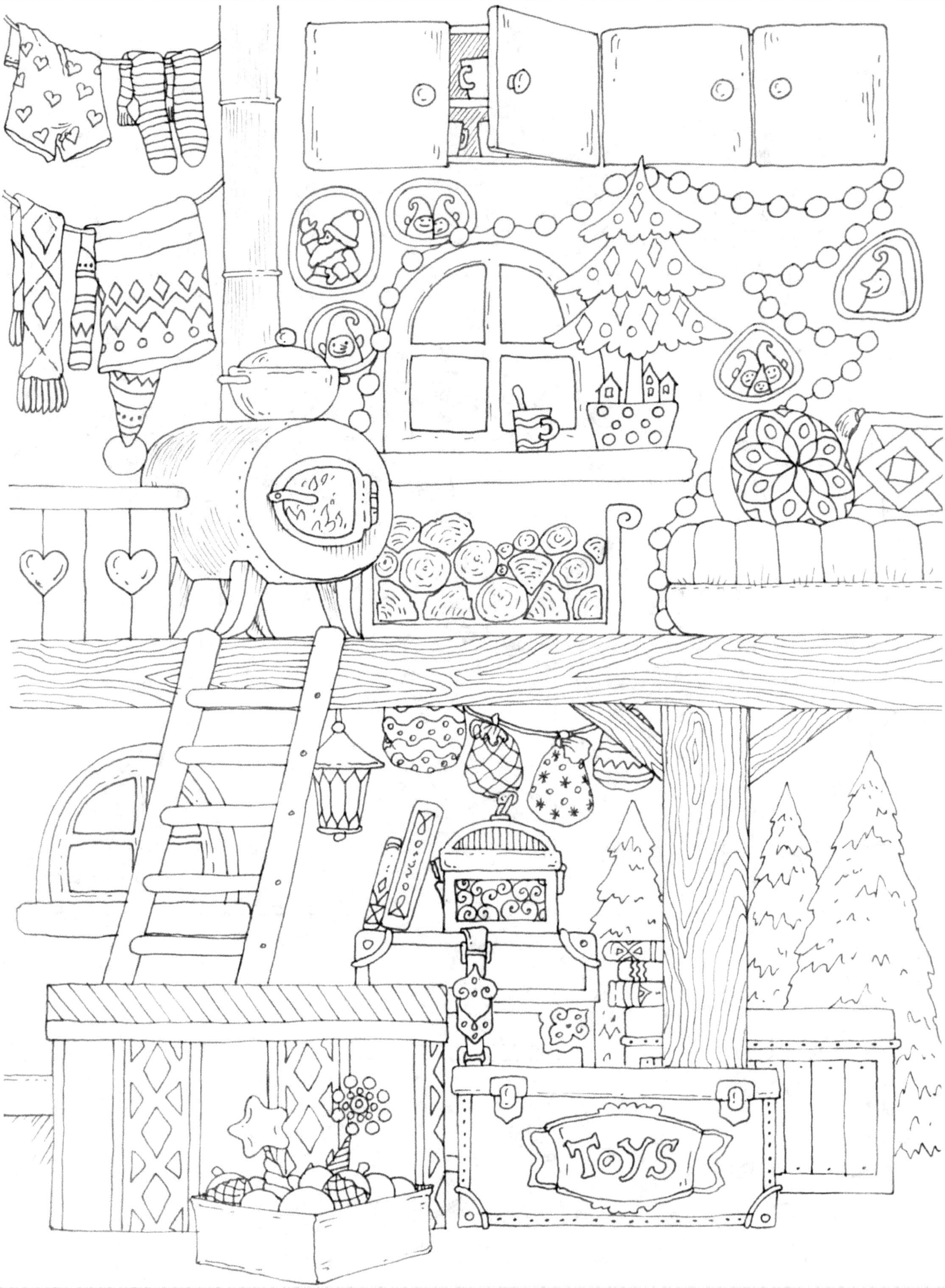
TOYS

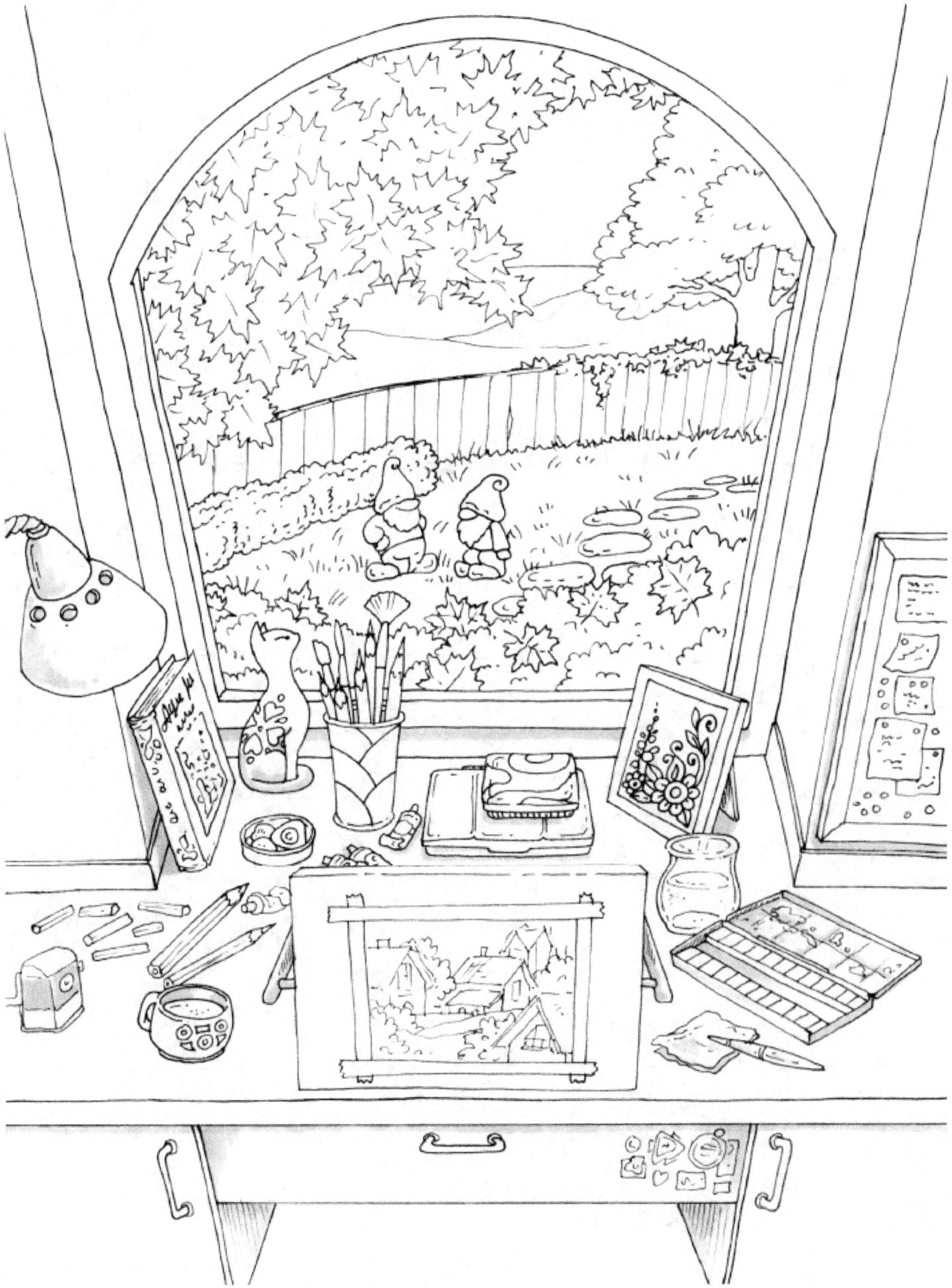

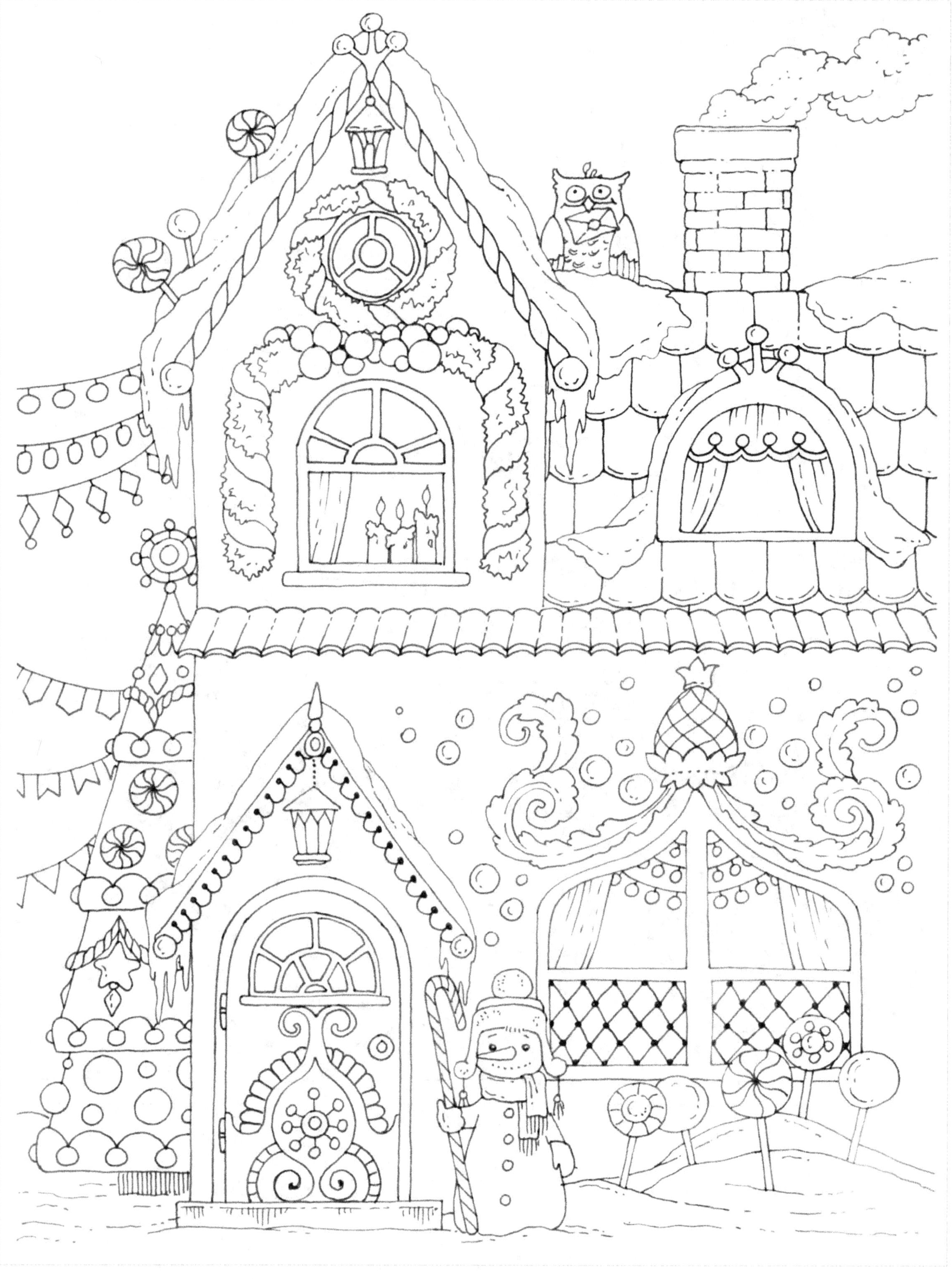

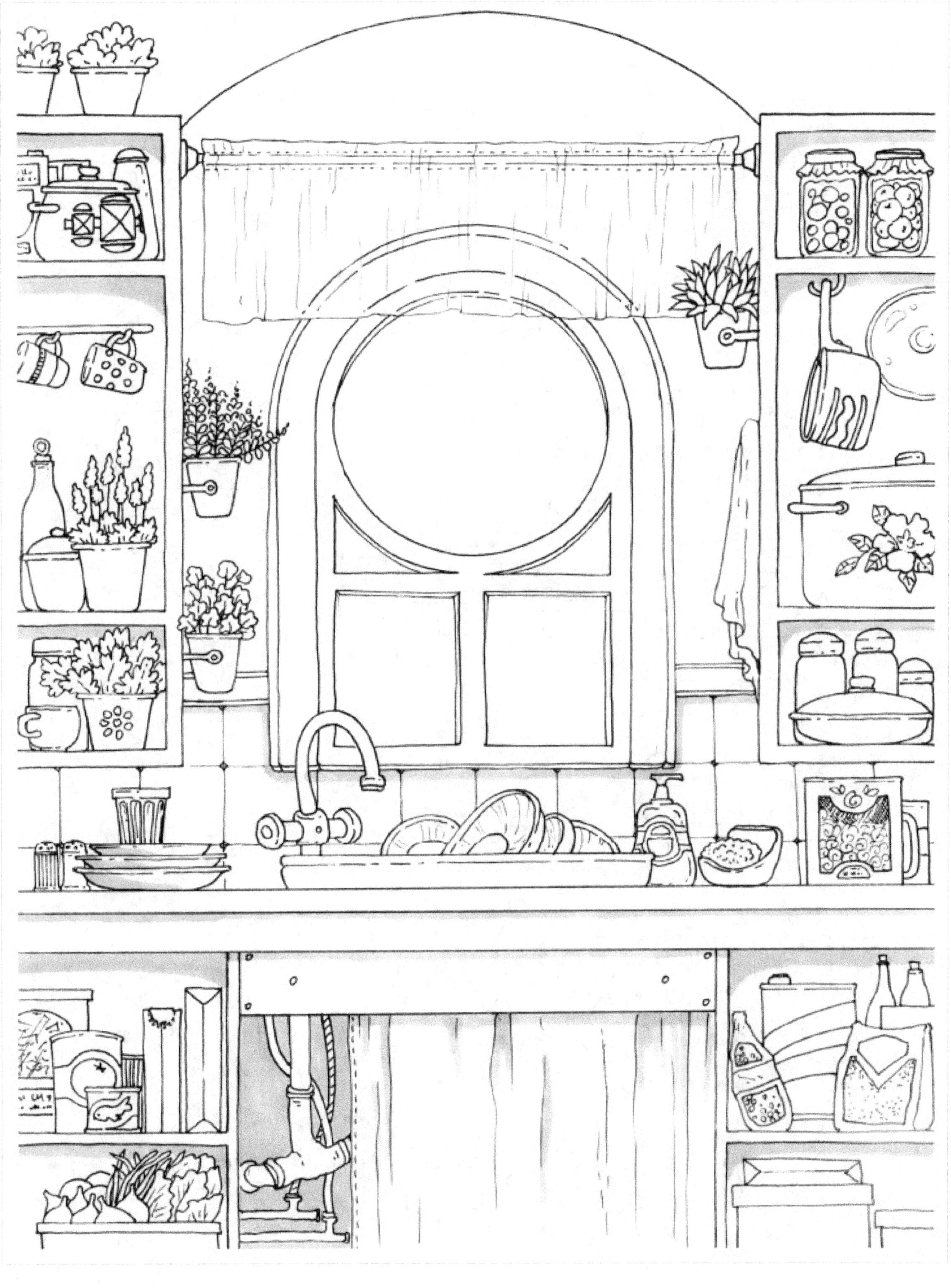

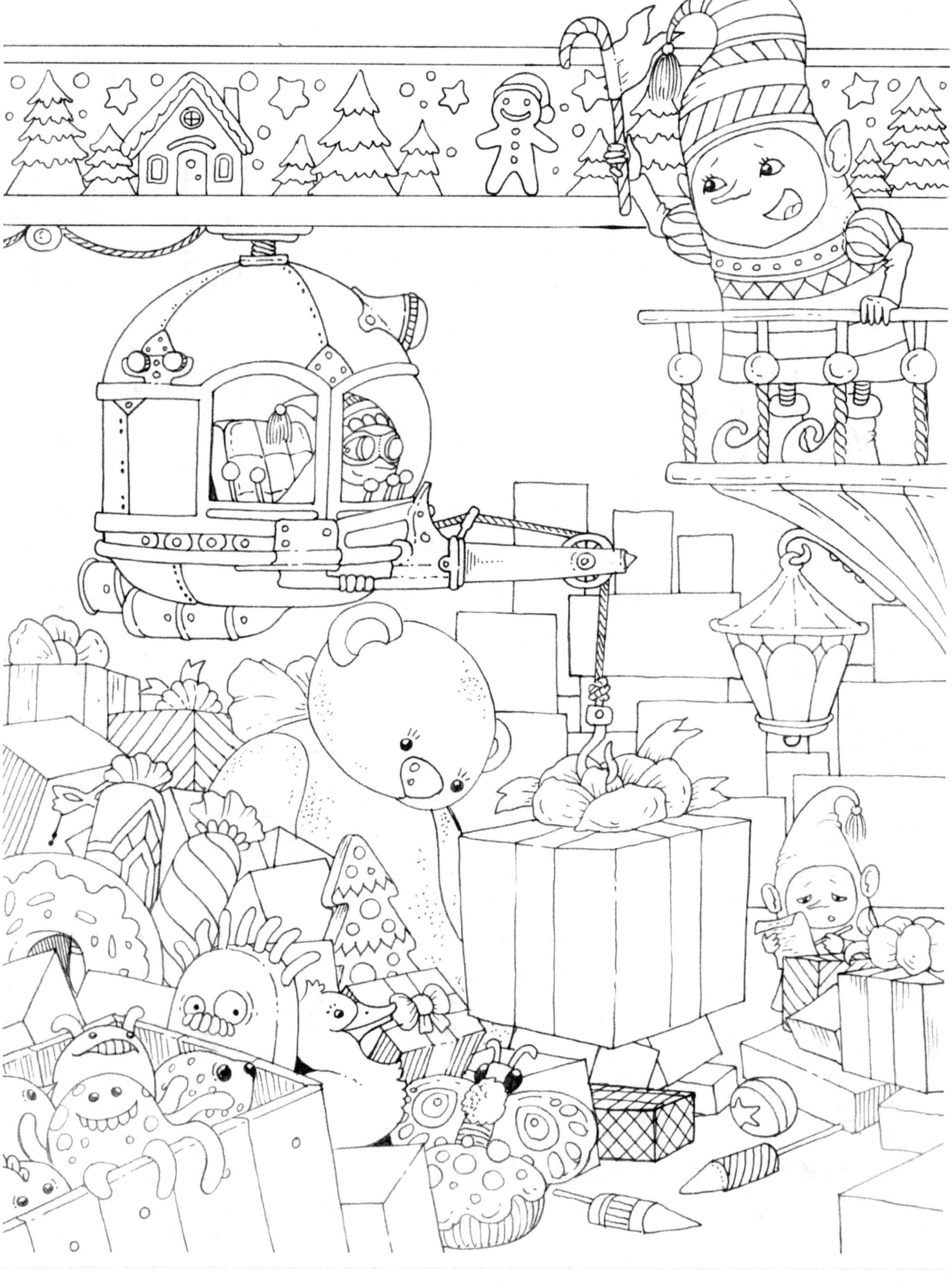

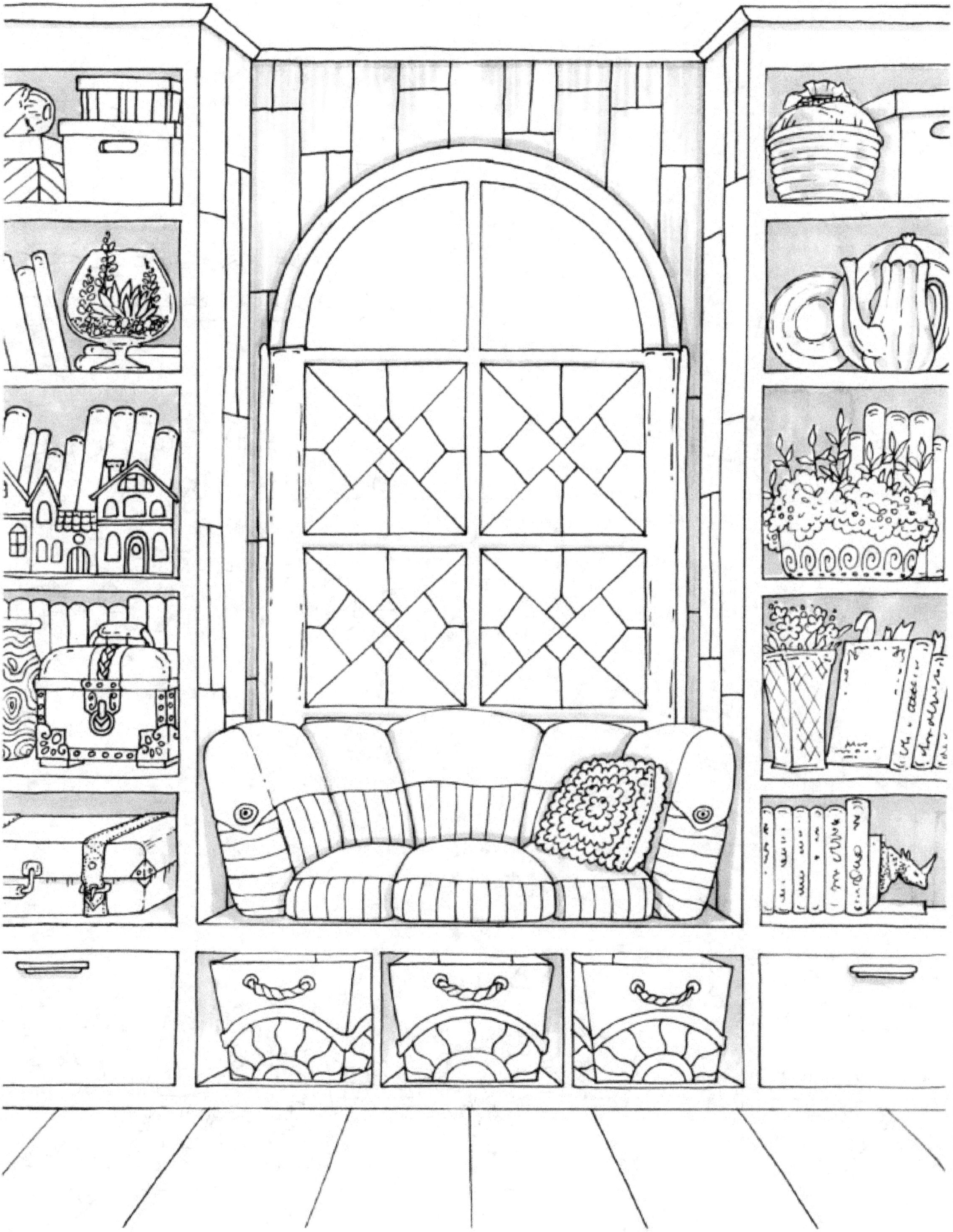

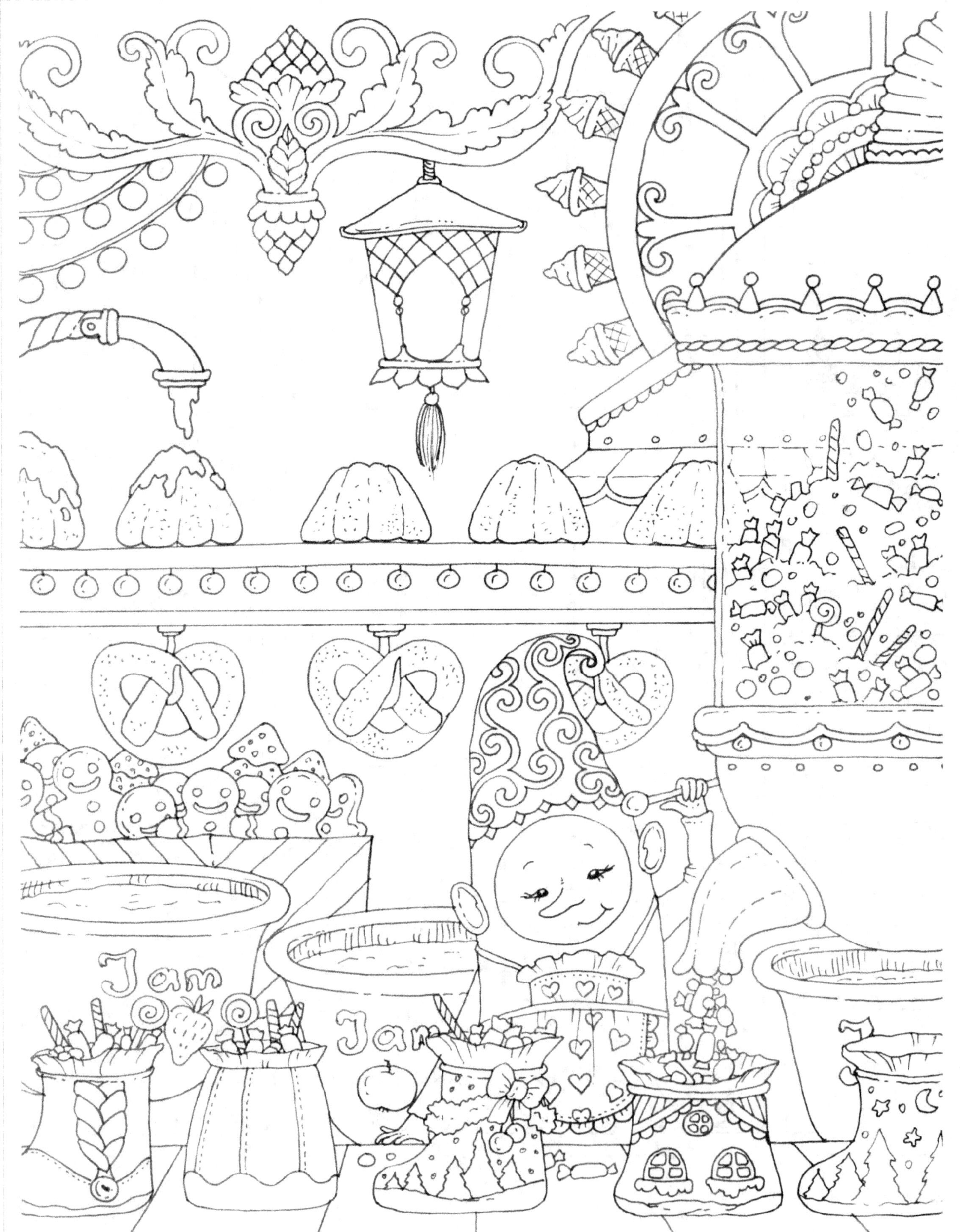
Jam
Jam

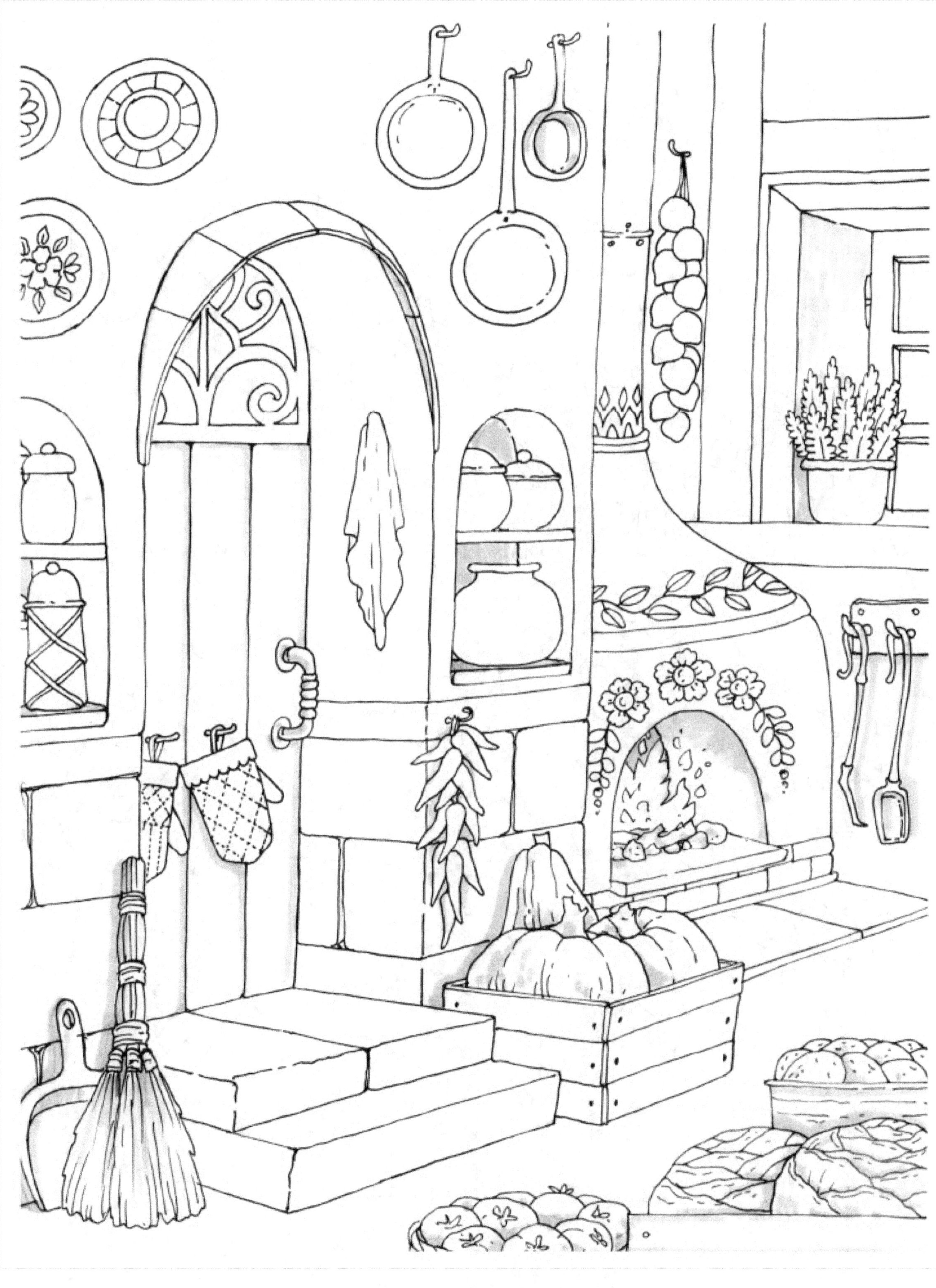

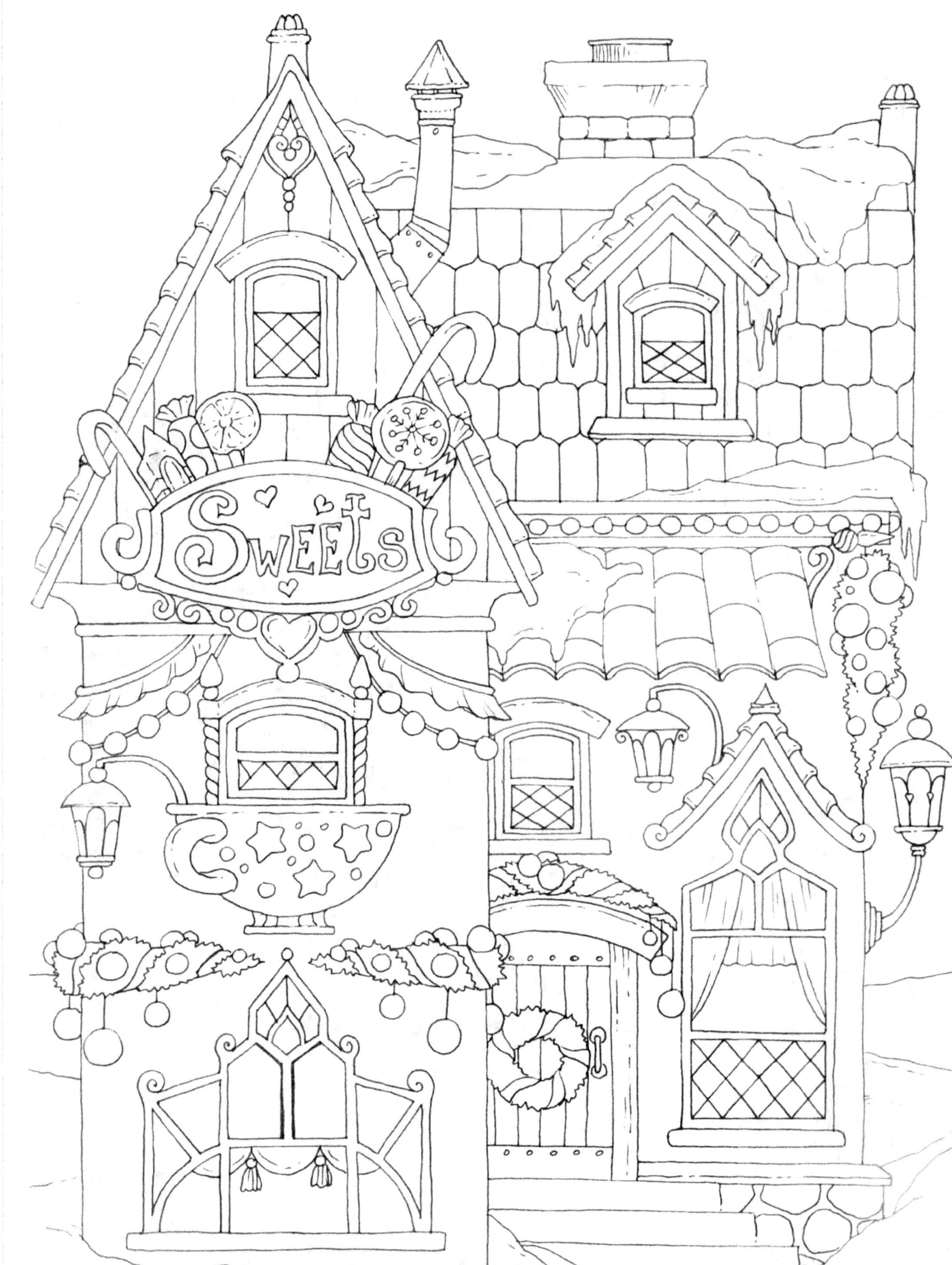
Sweets

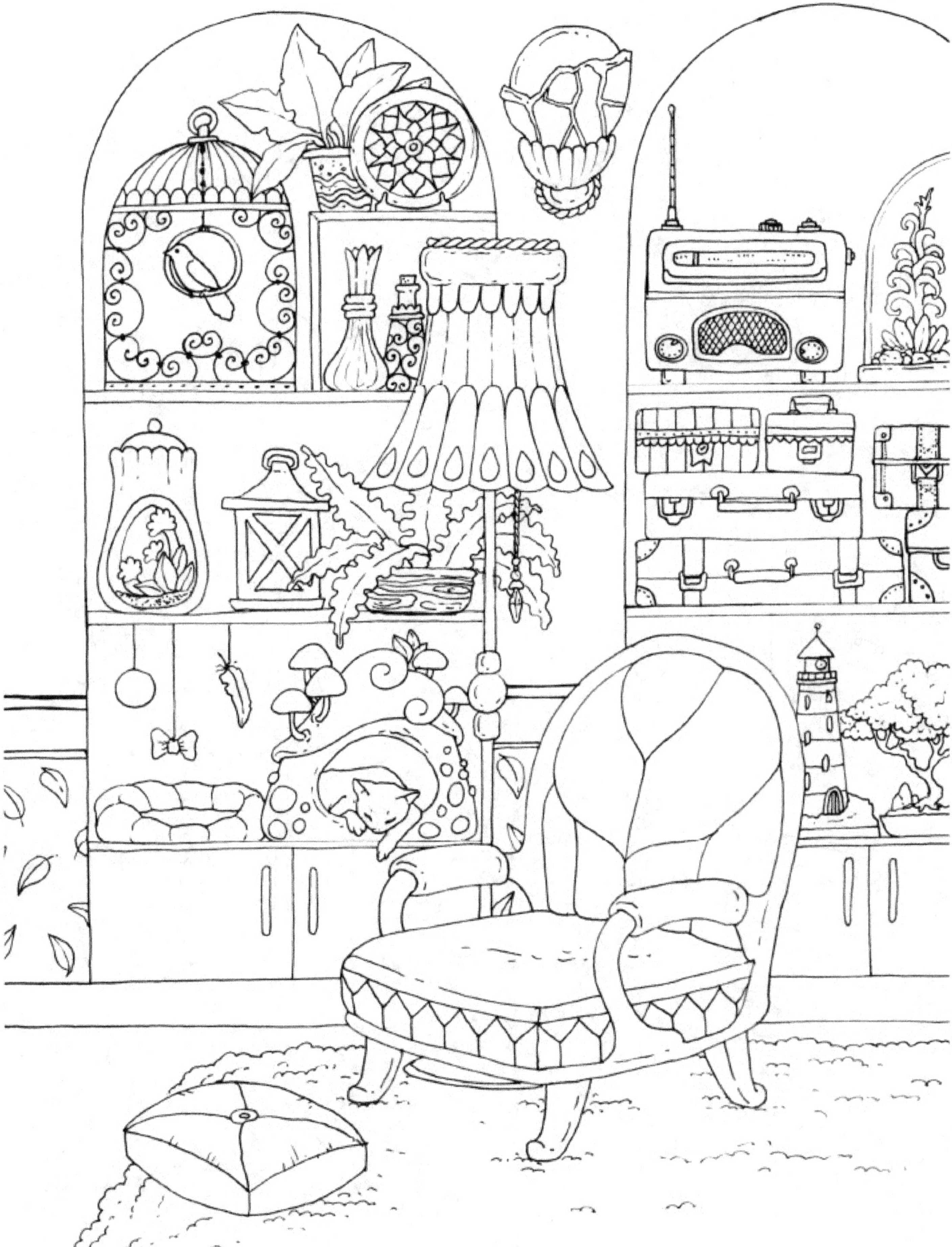

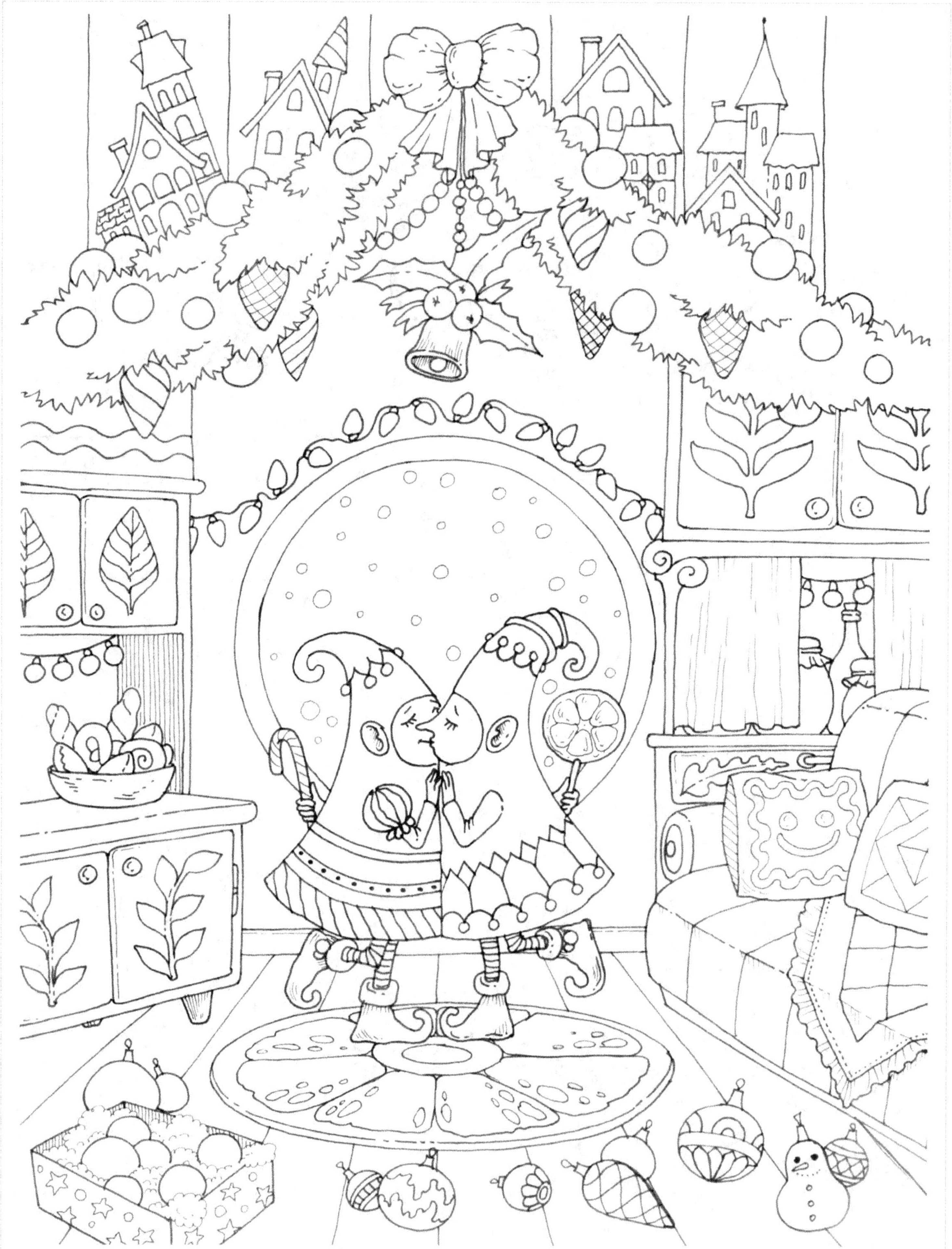

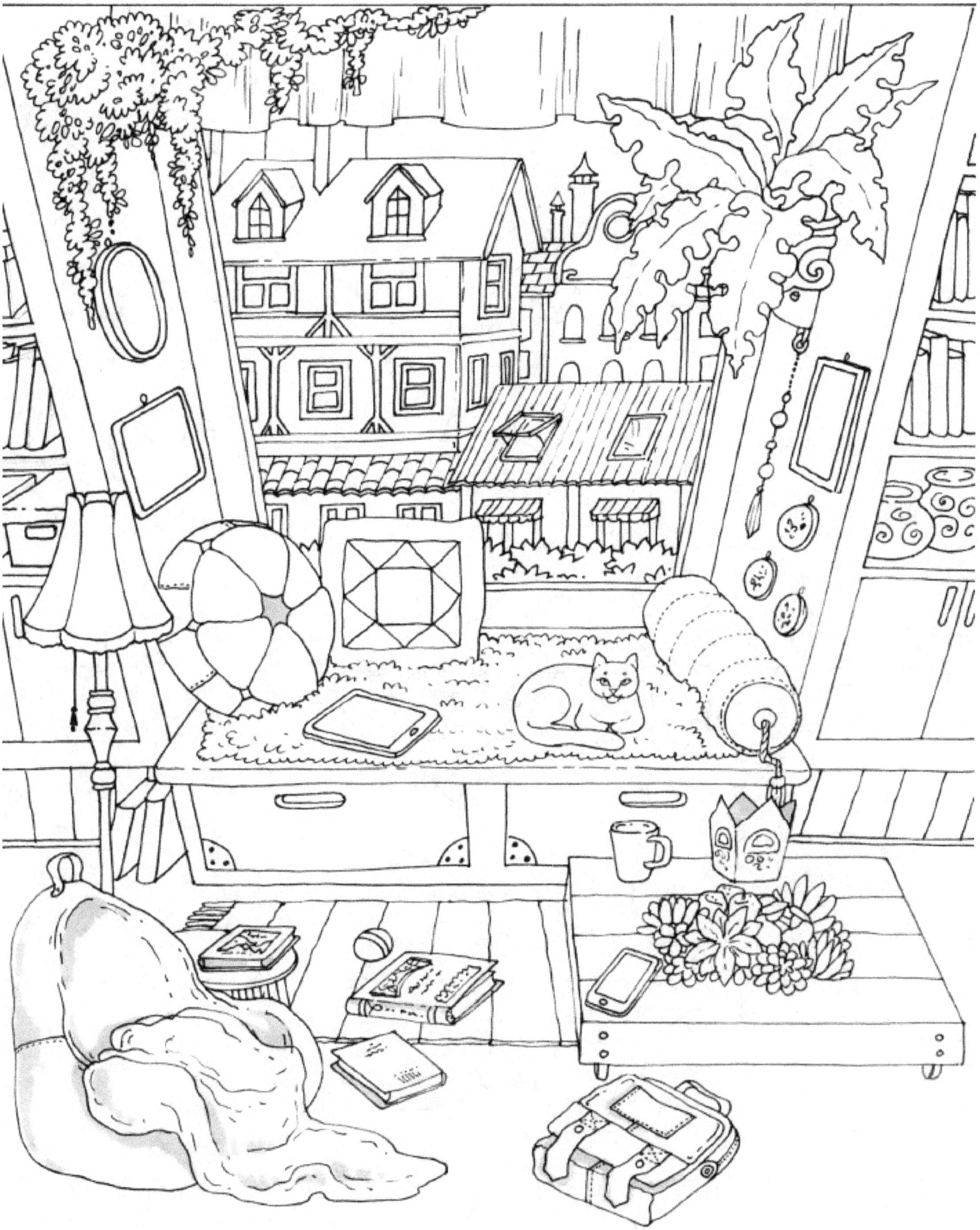

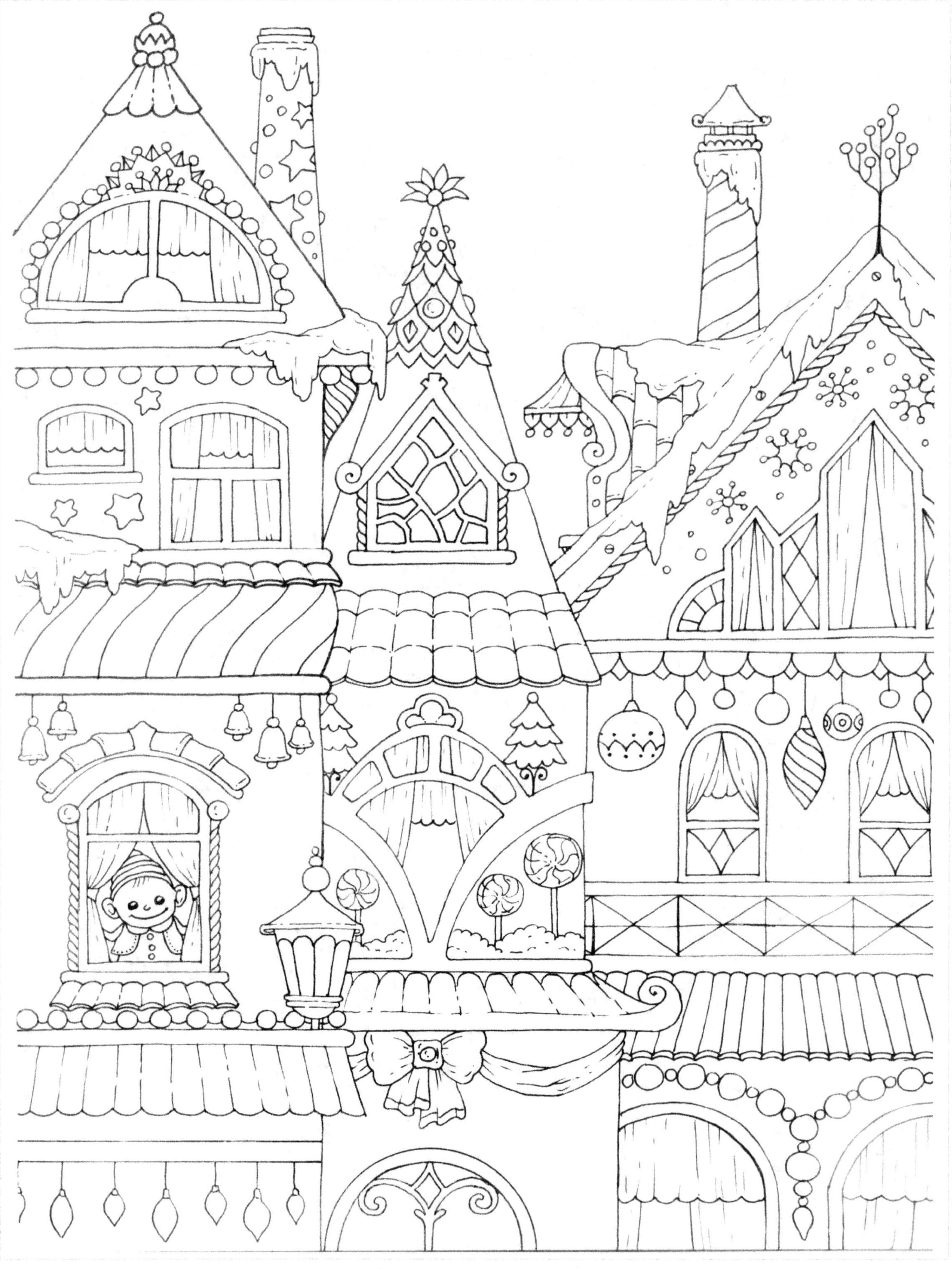

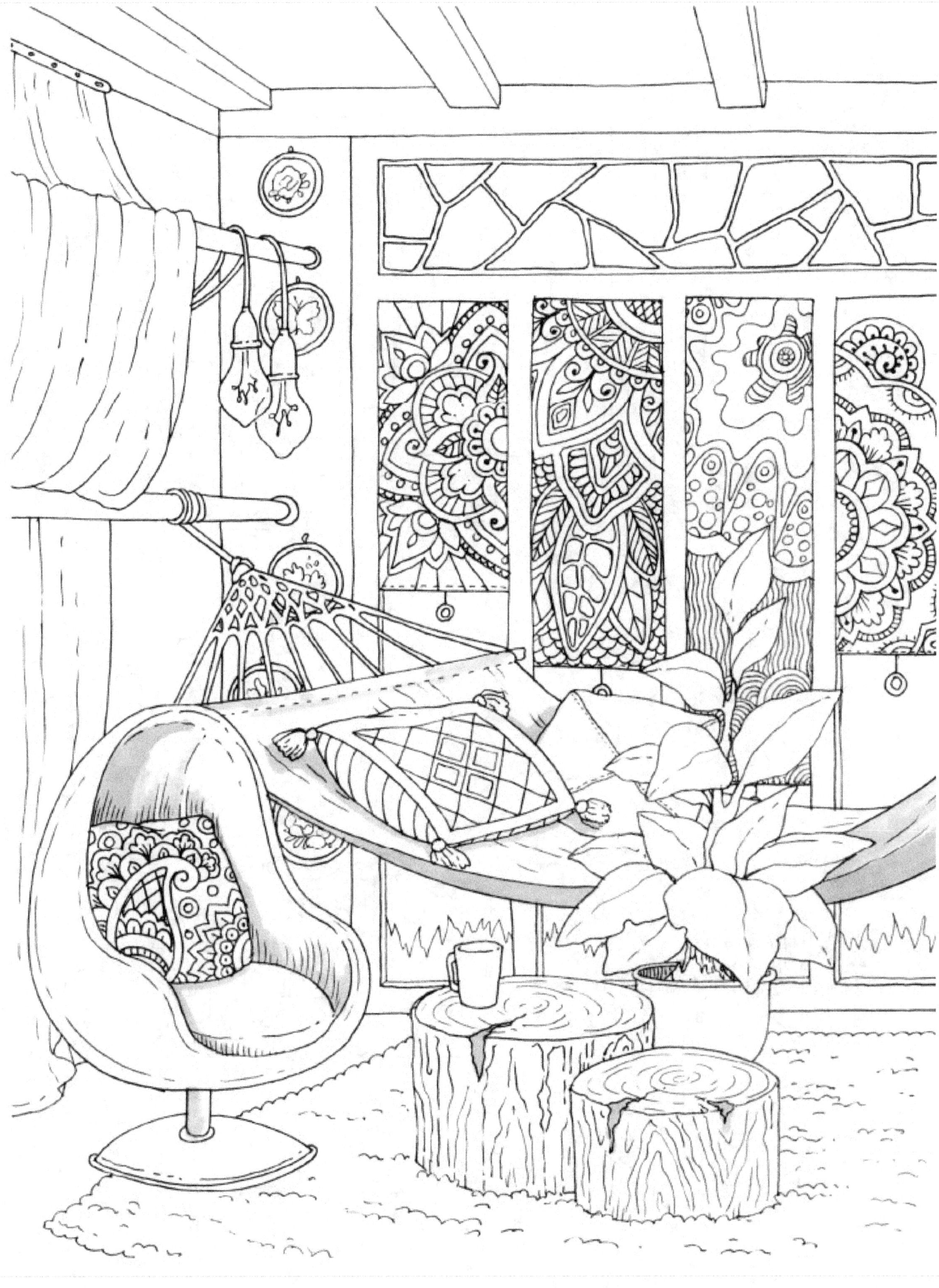

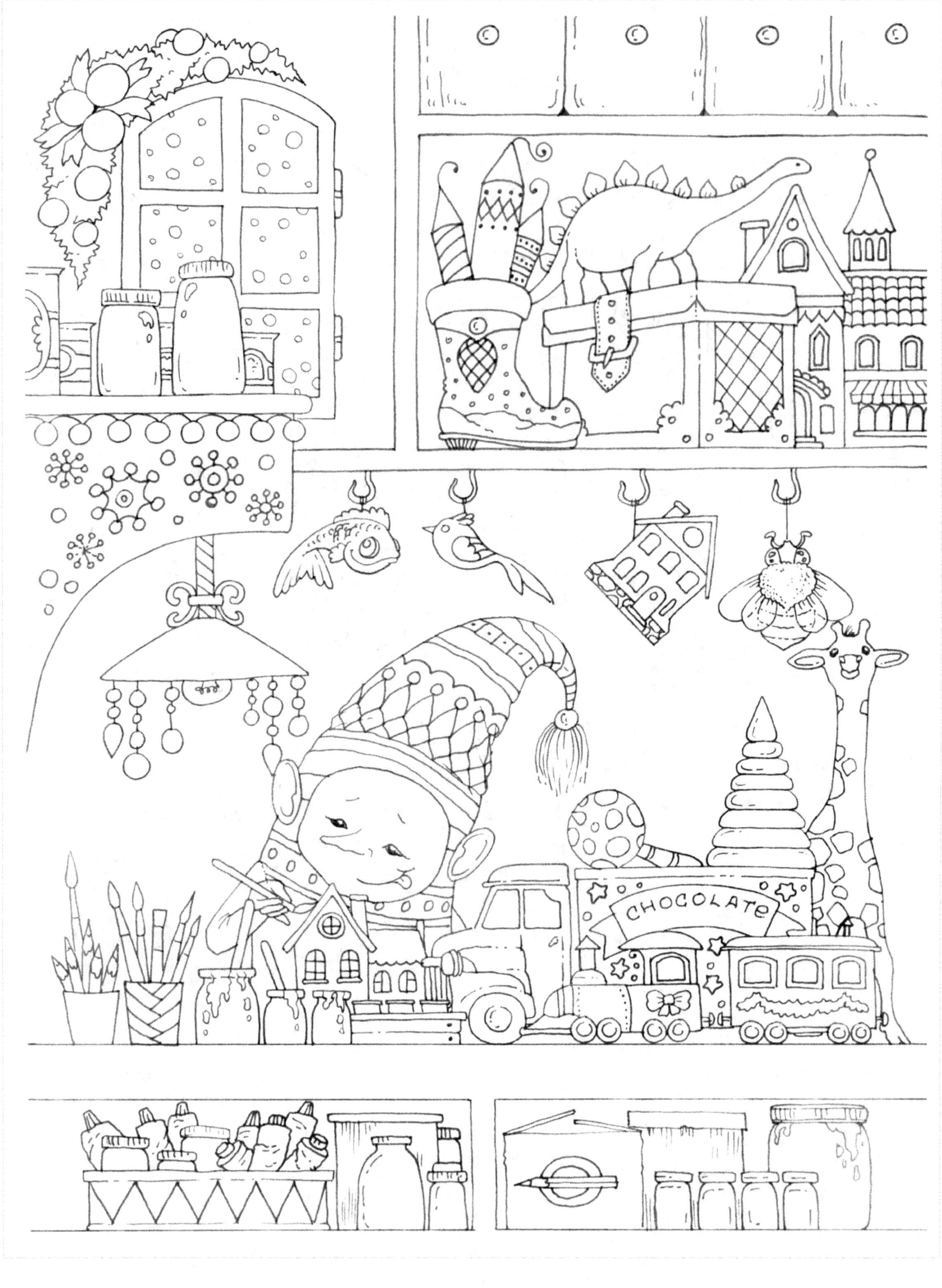
CHOCOLATE

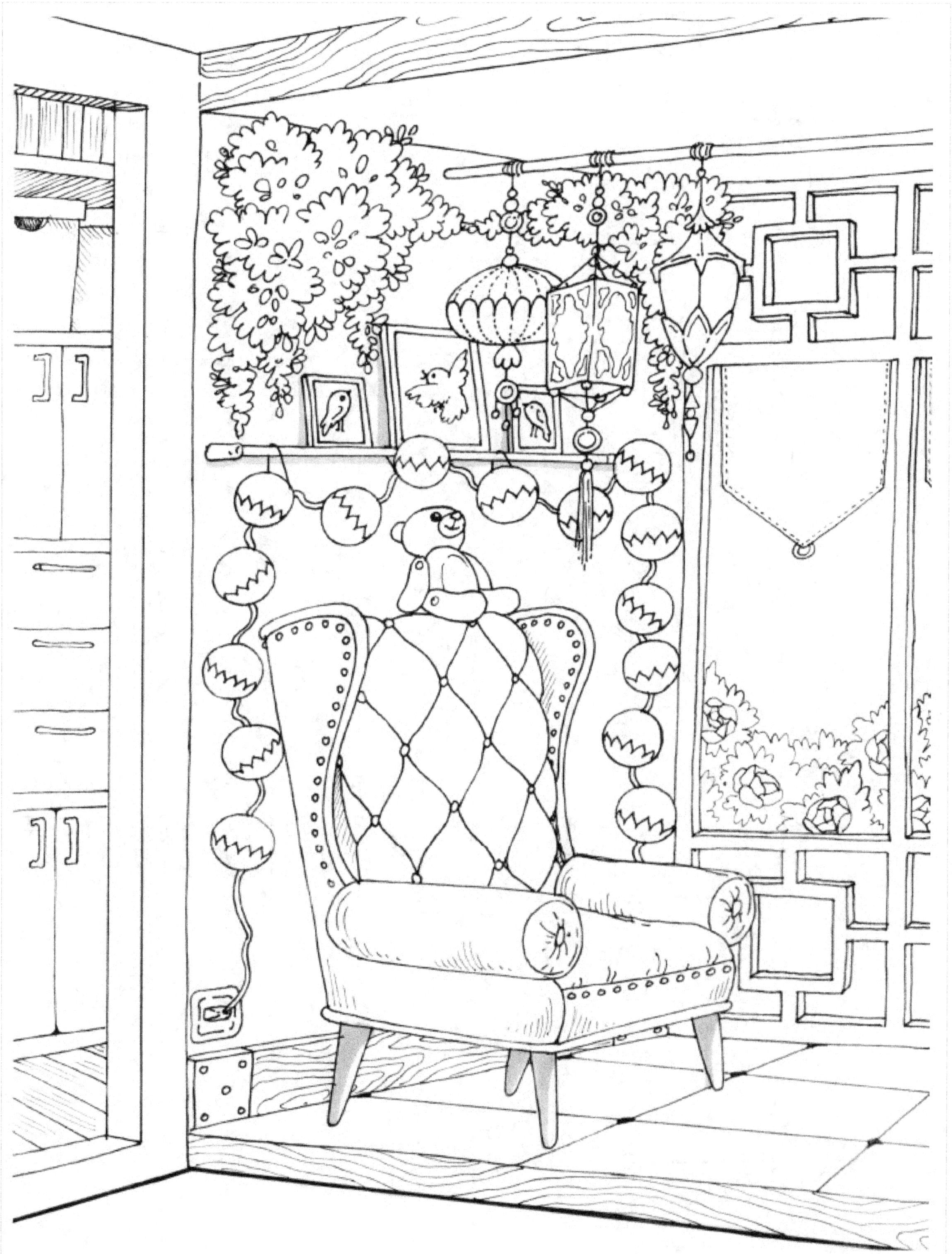

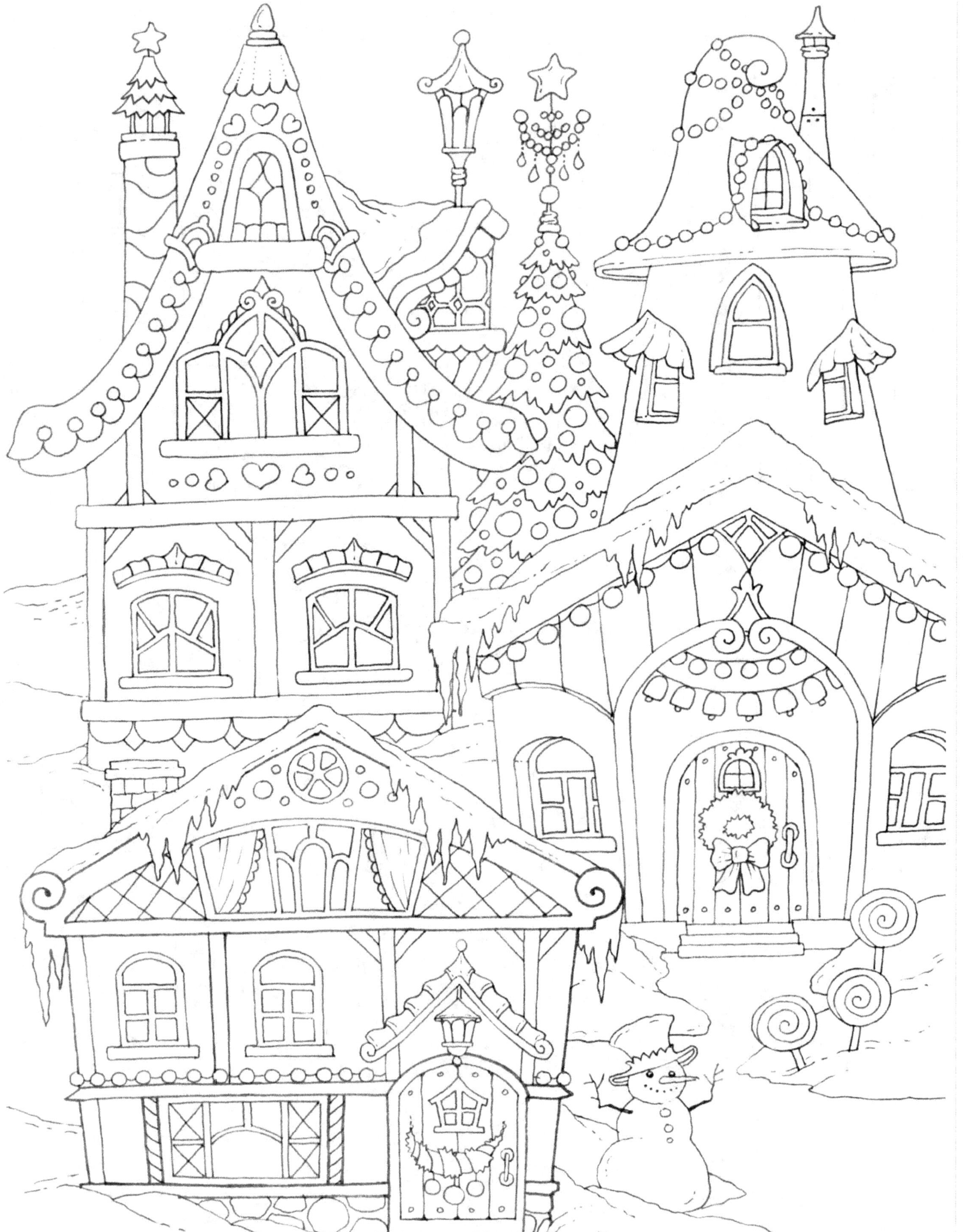

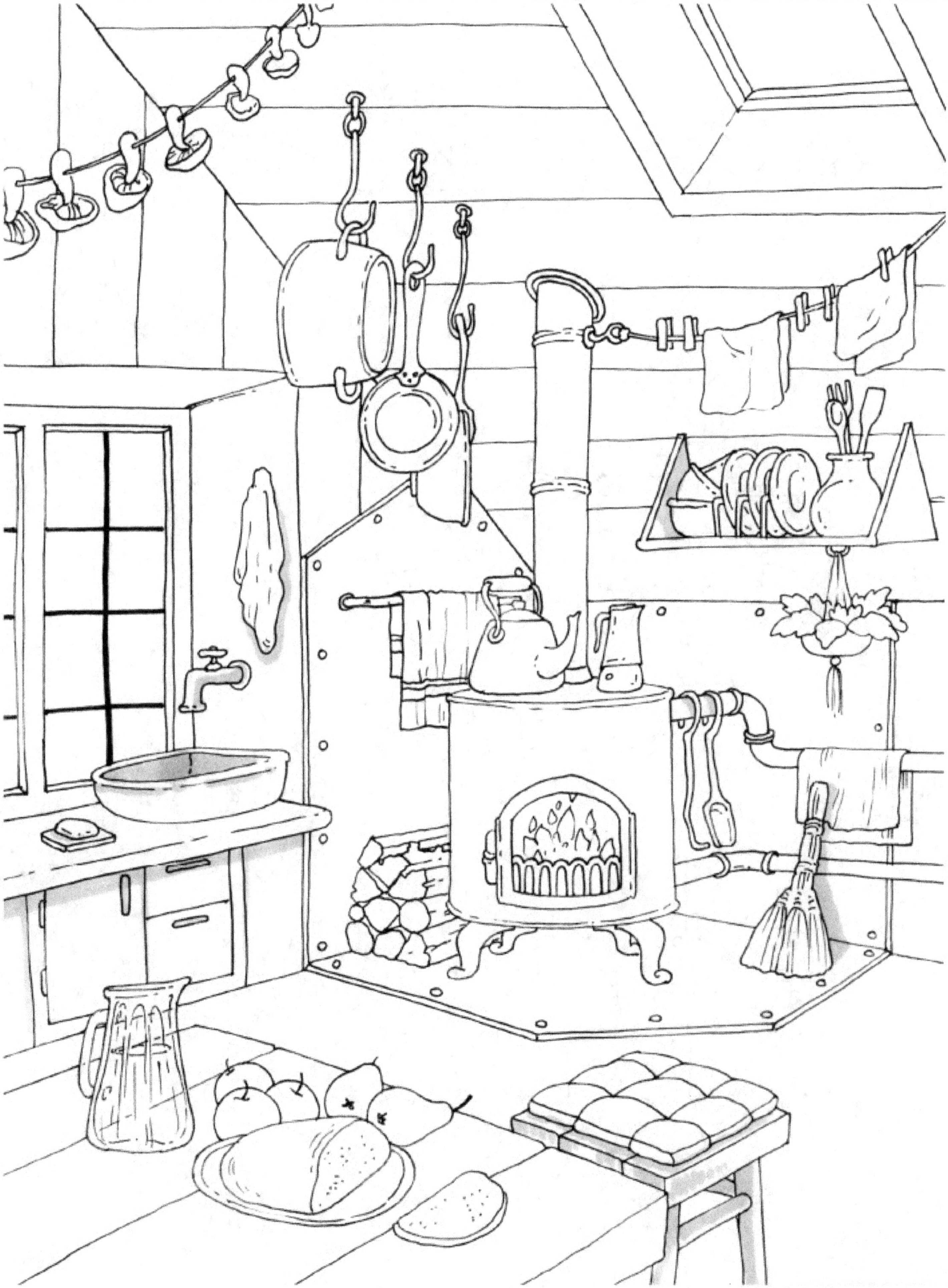

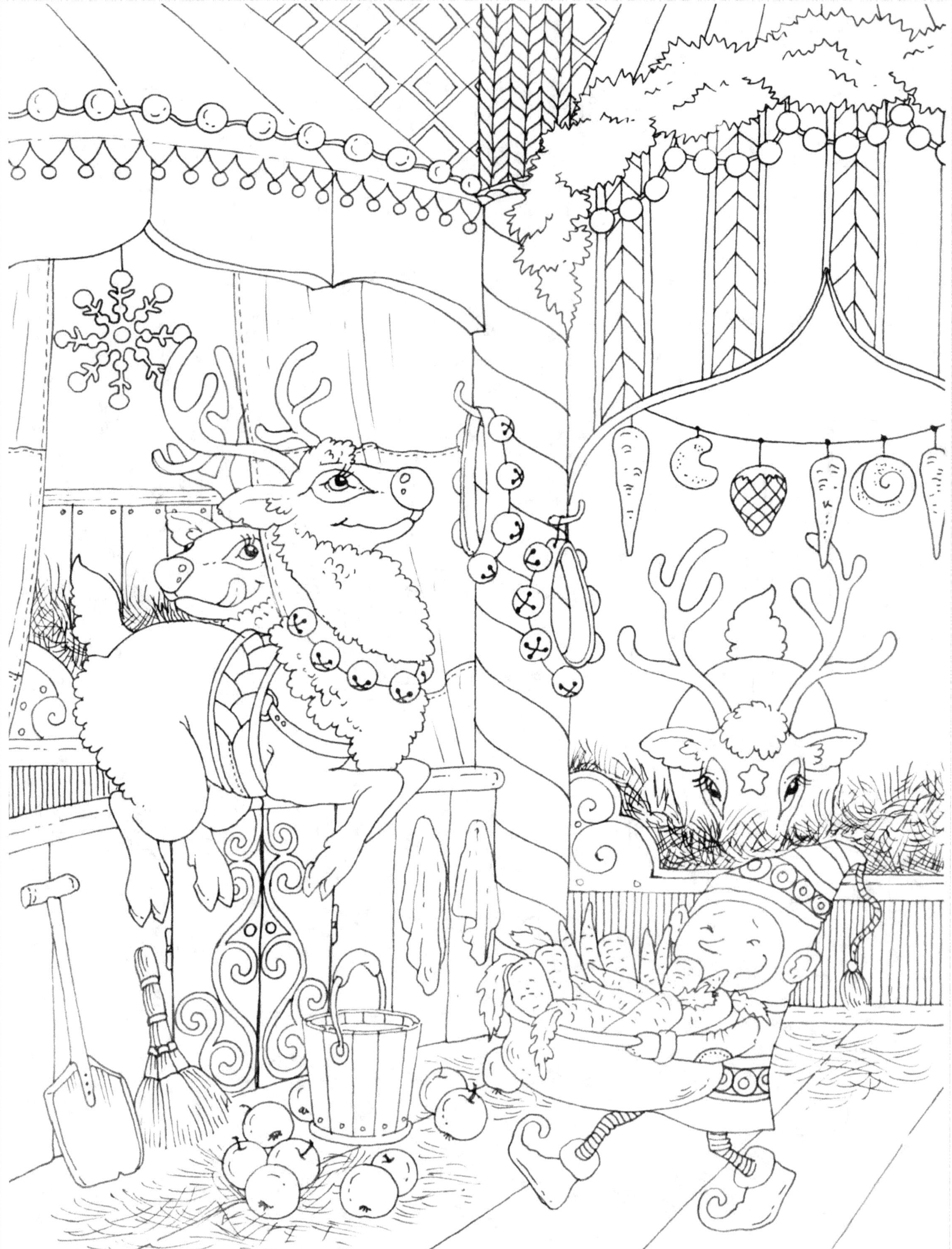

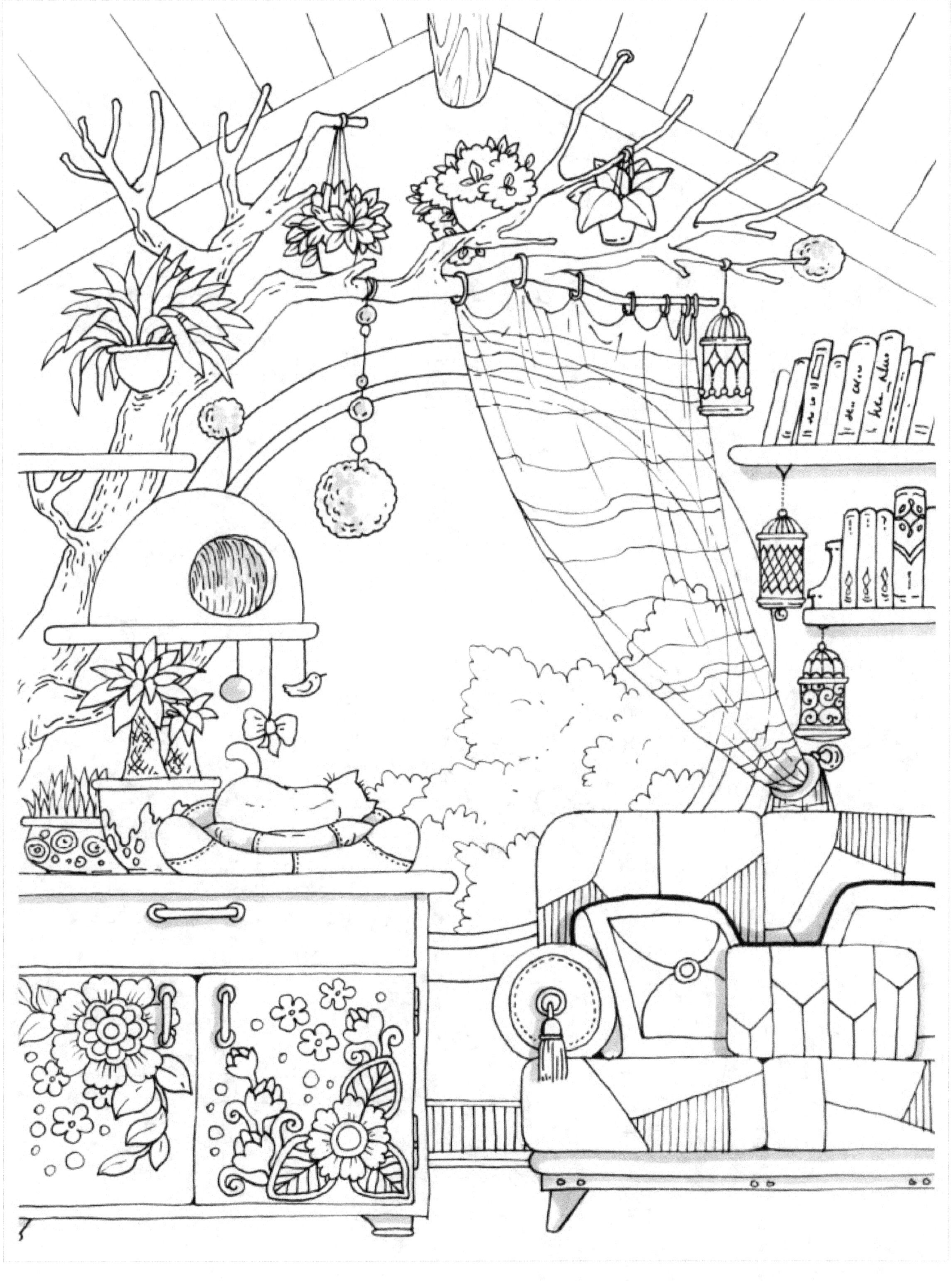

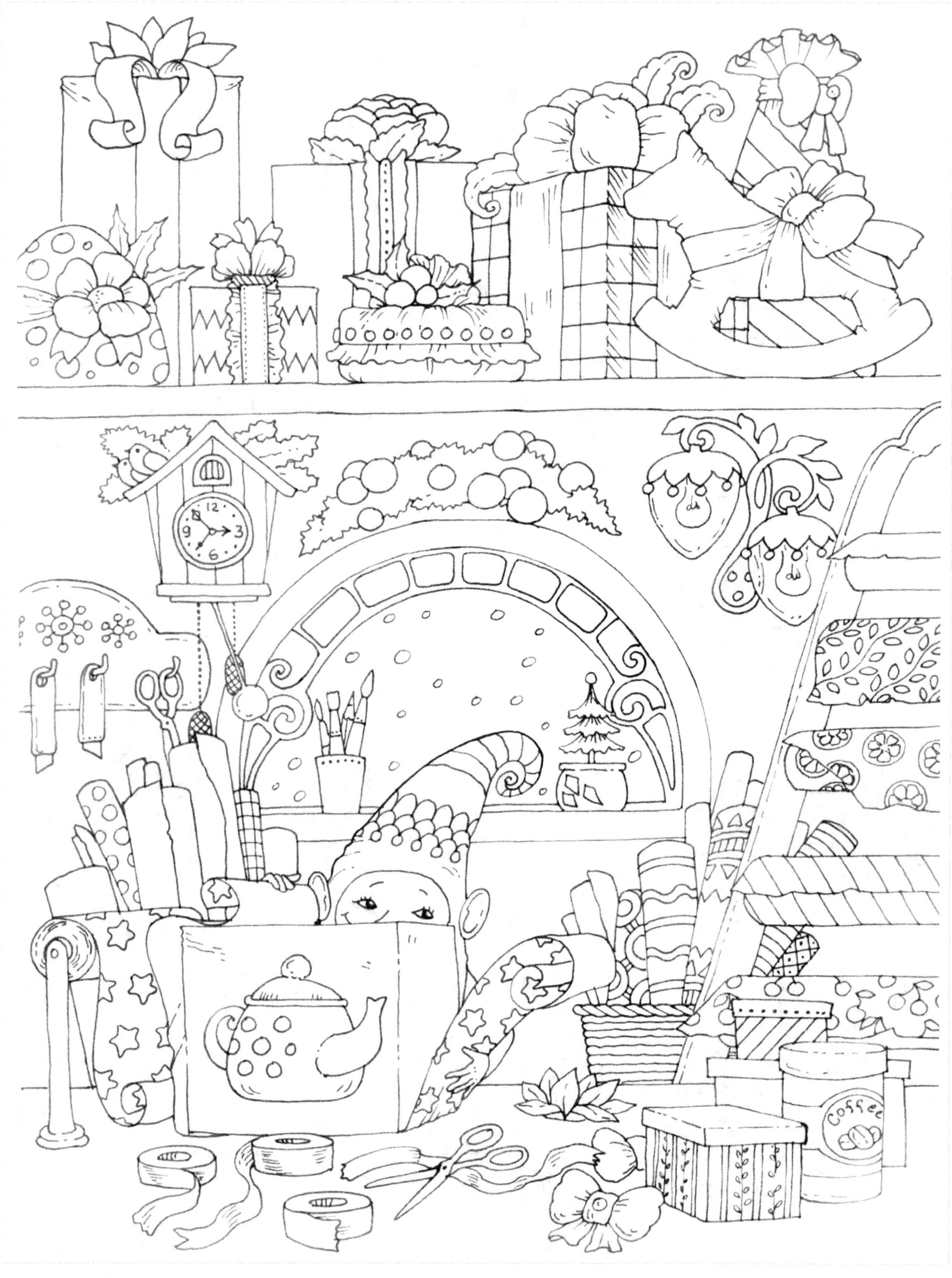
coffee

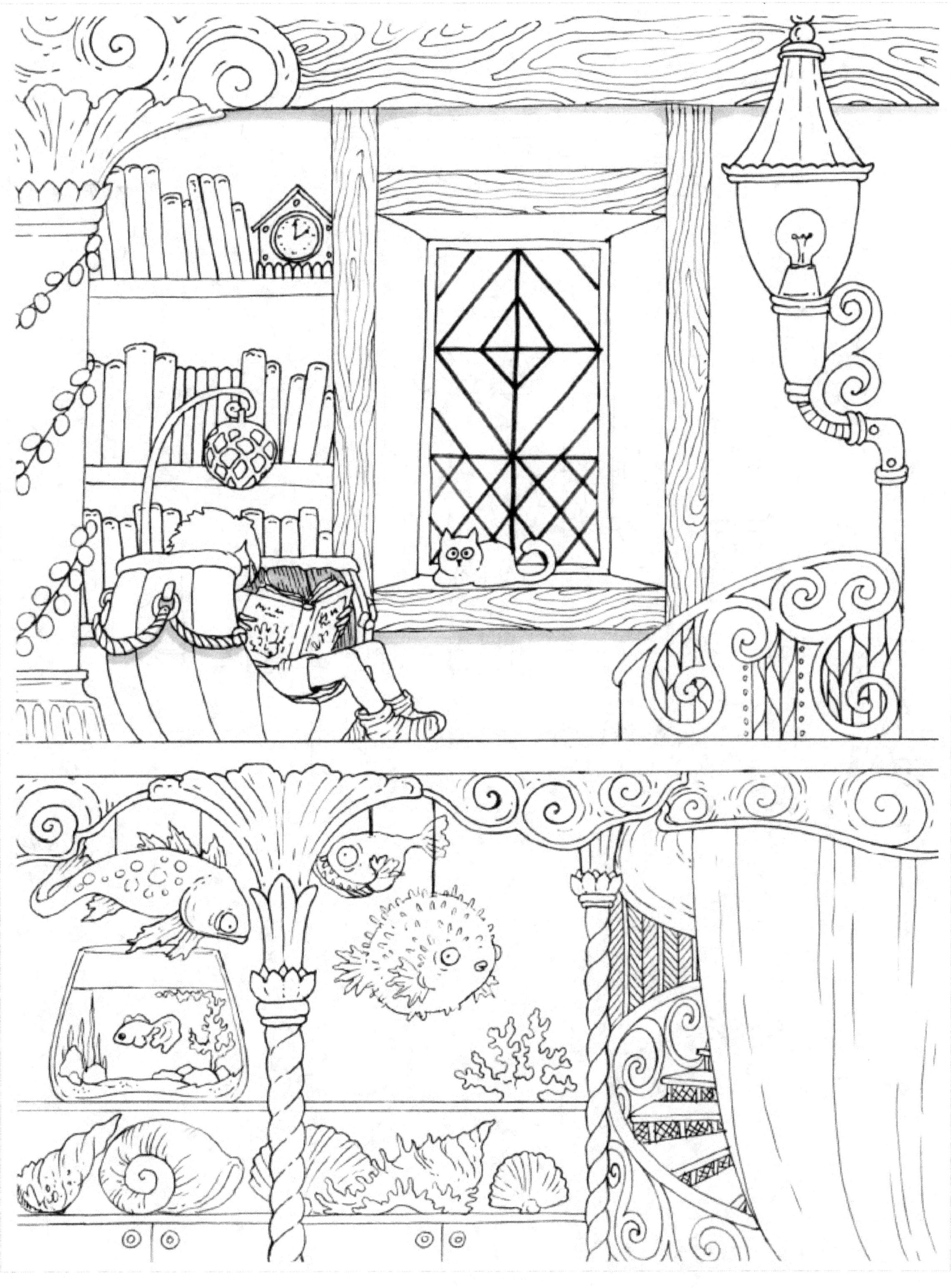

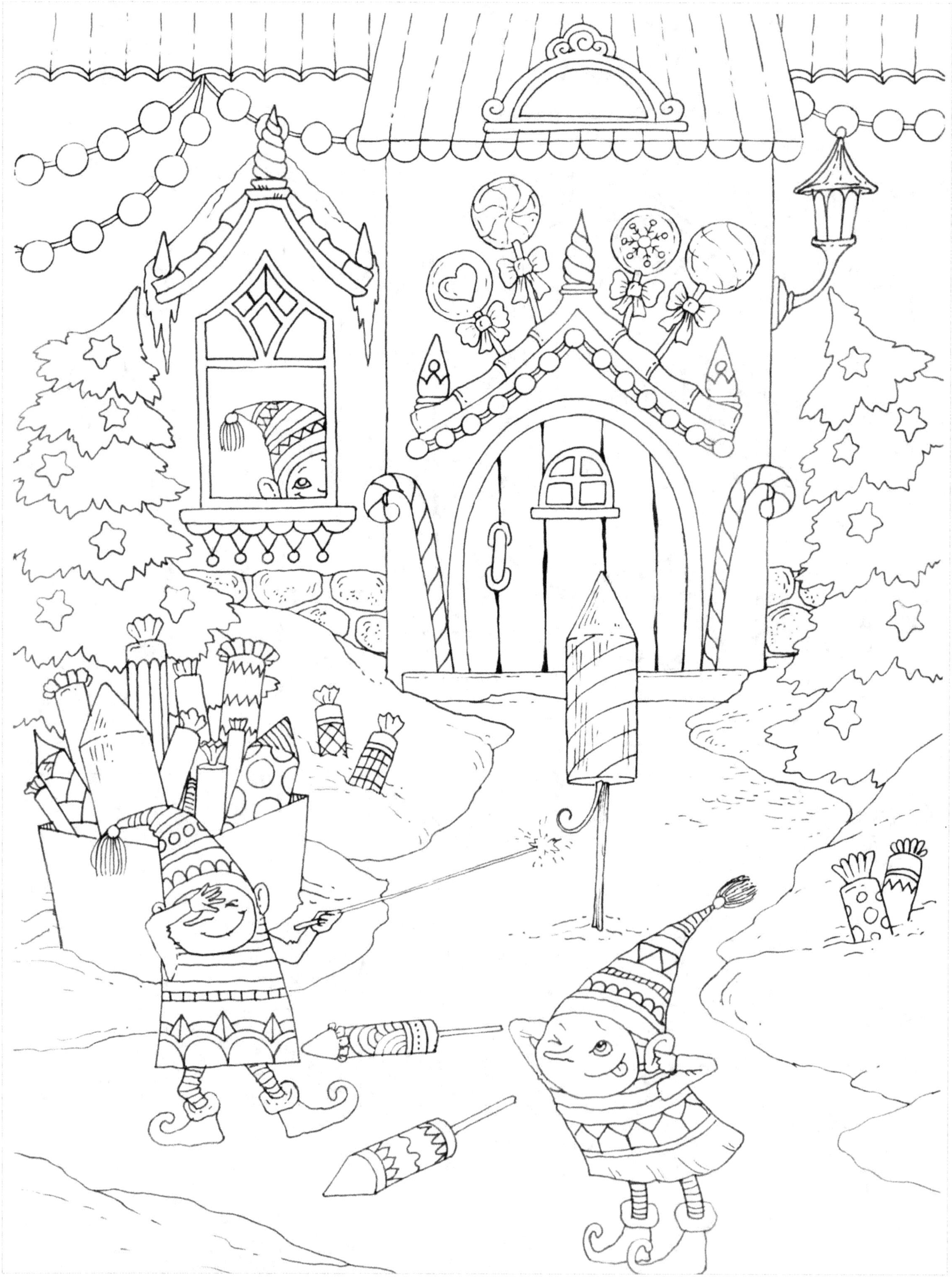

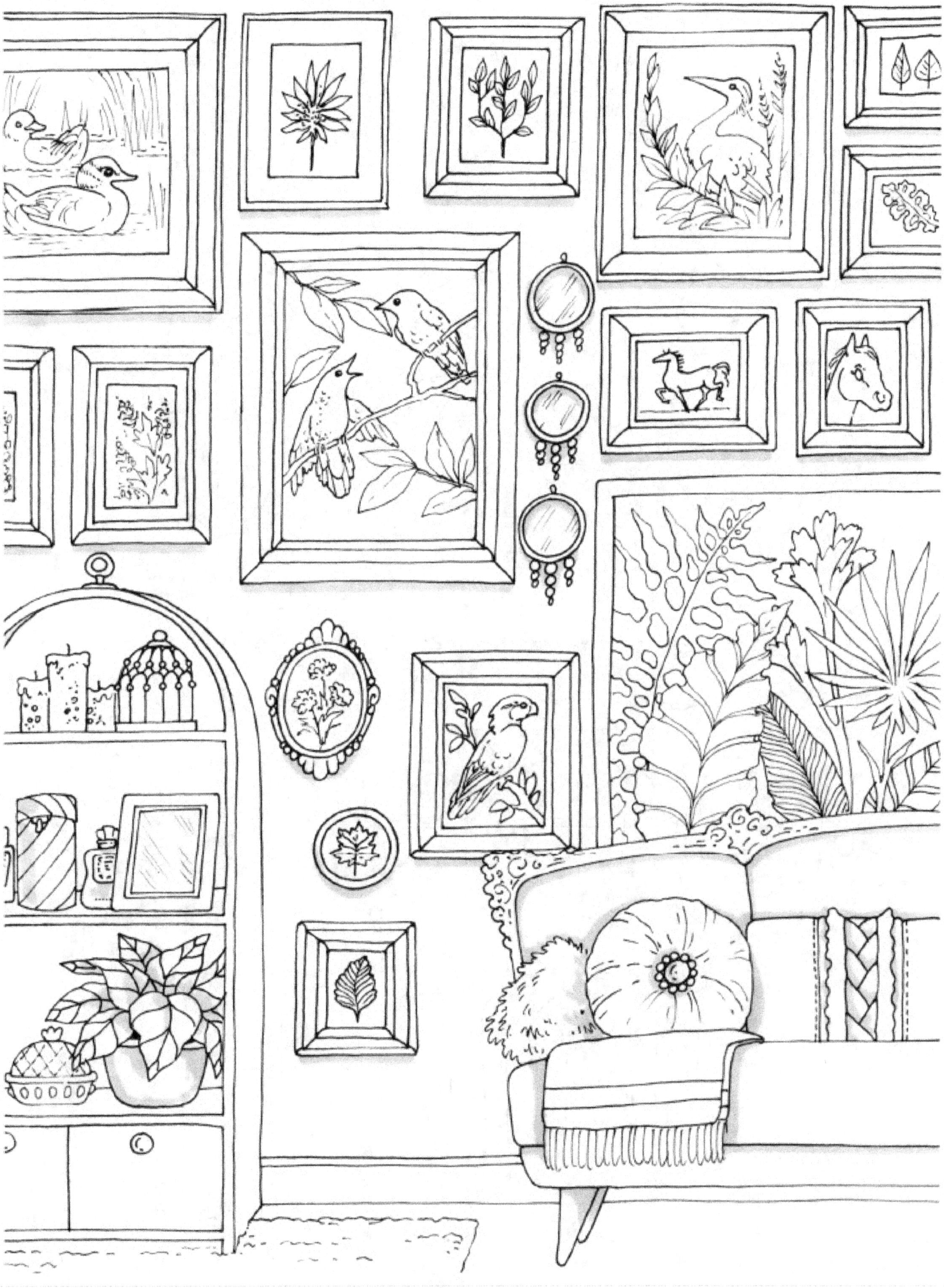

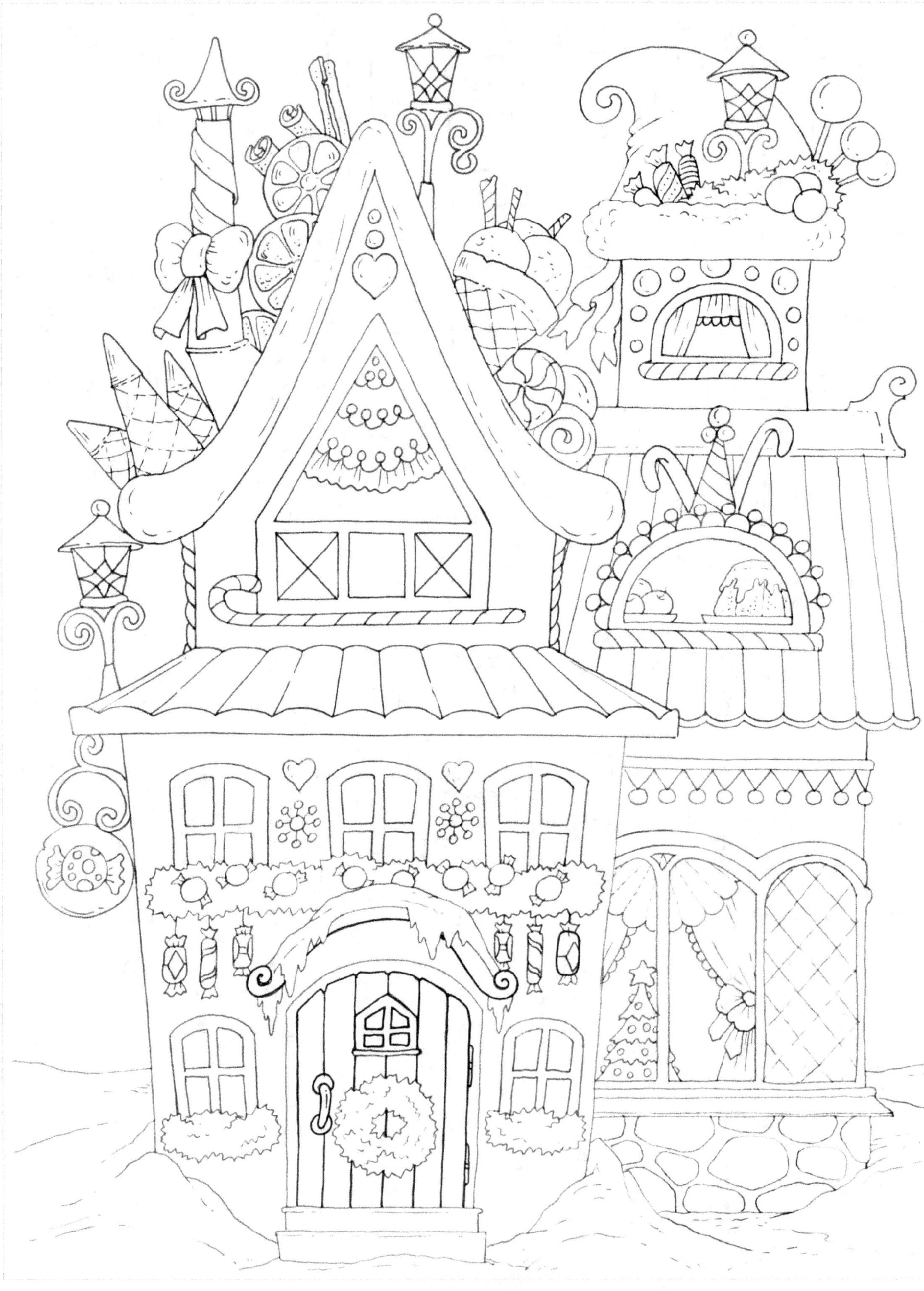

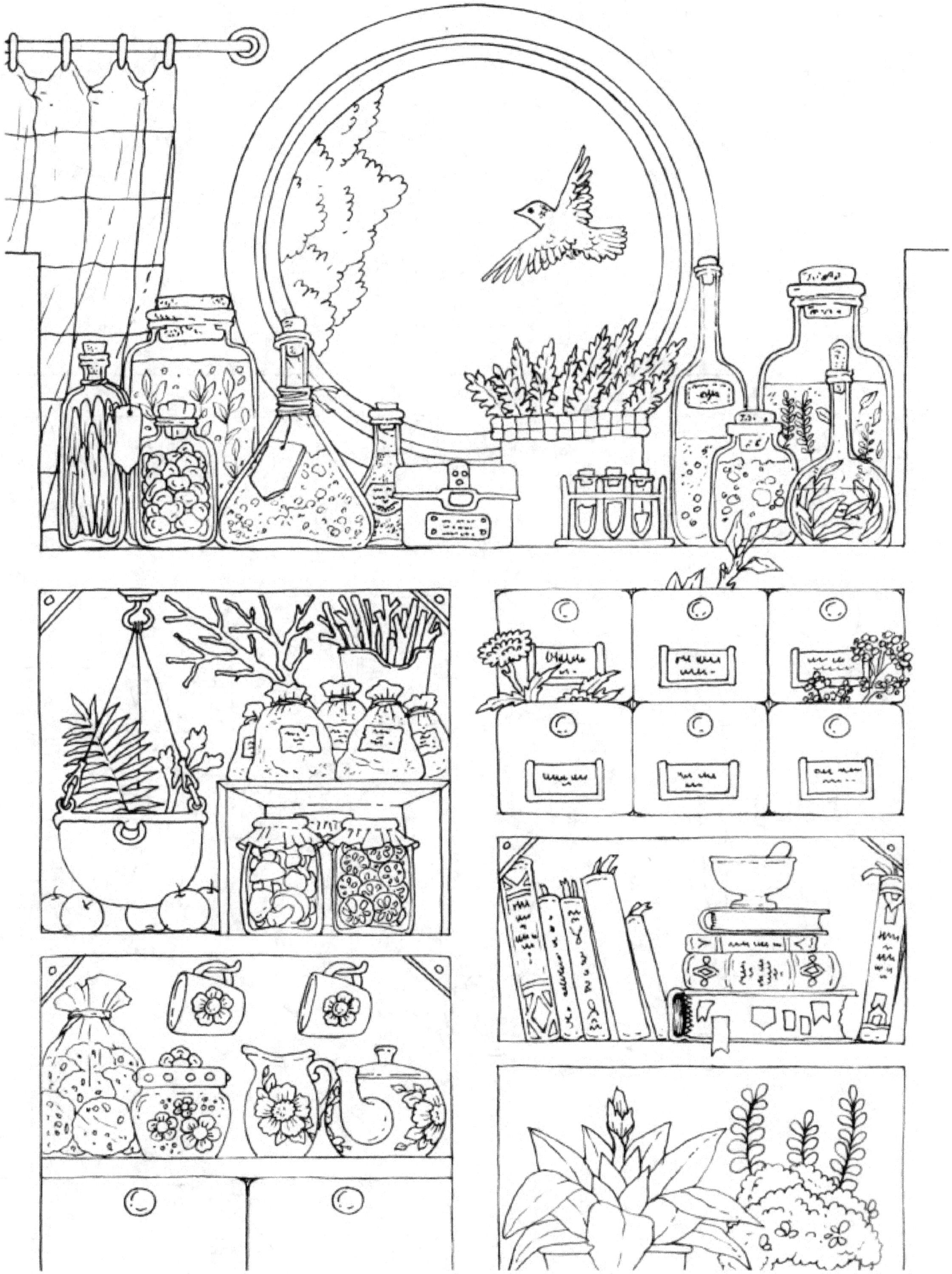

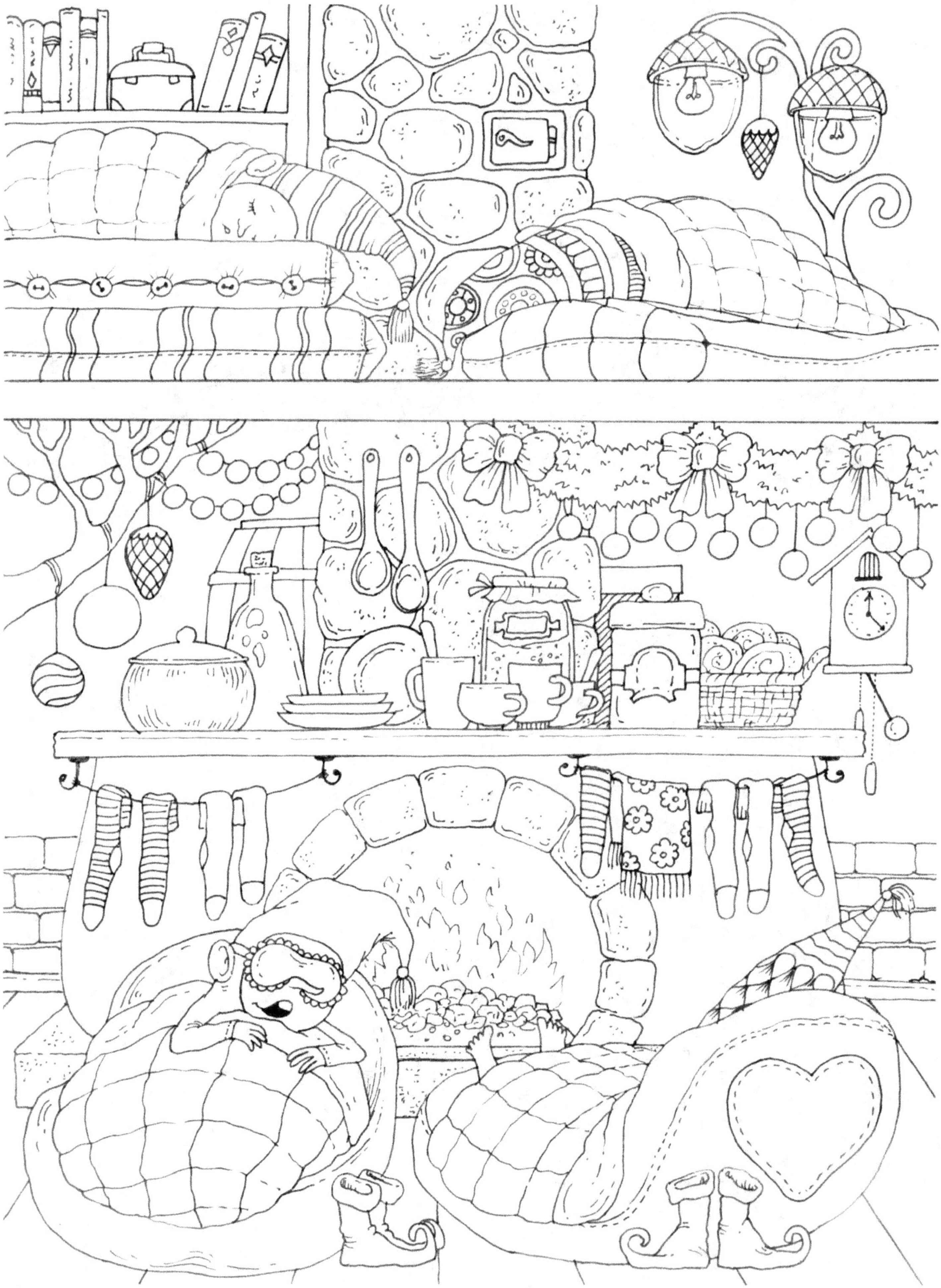

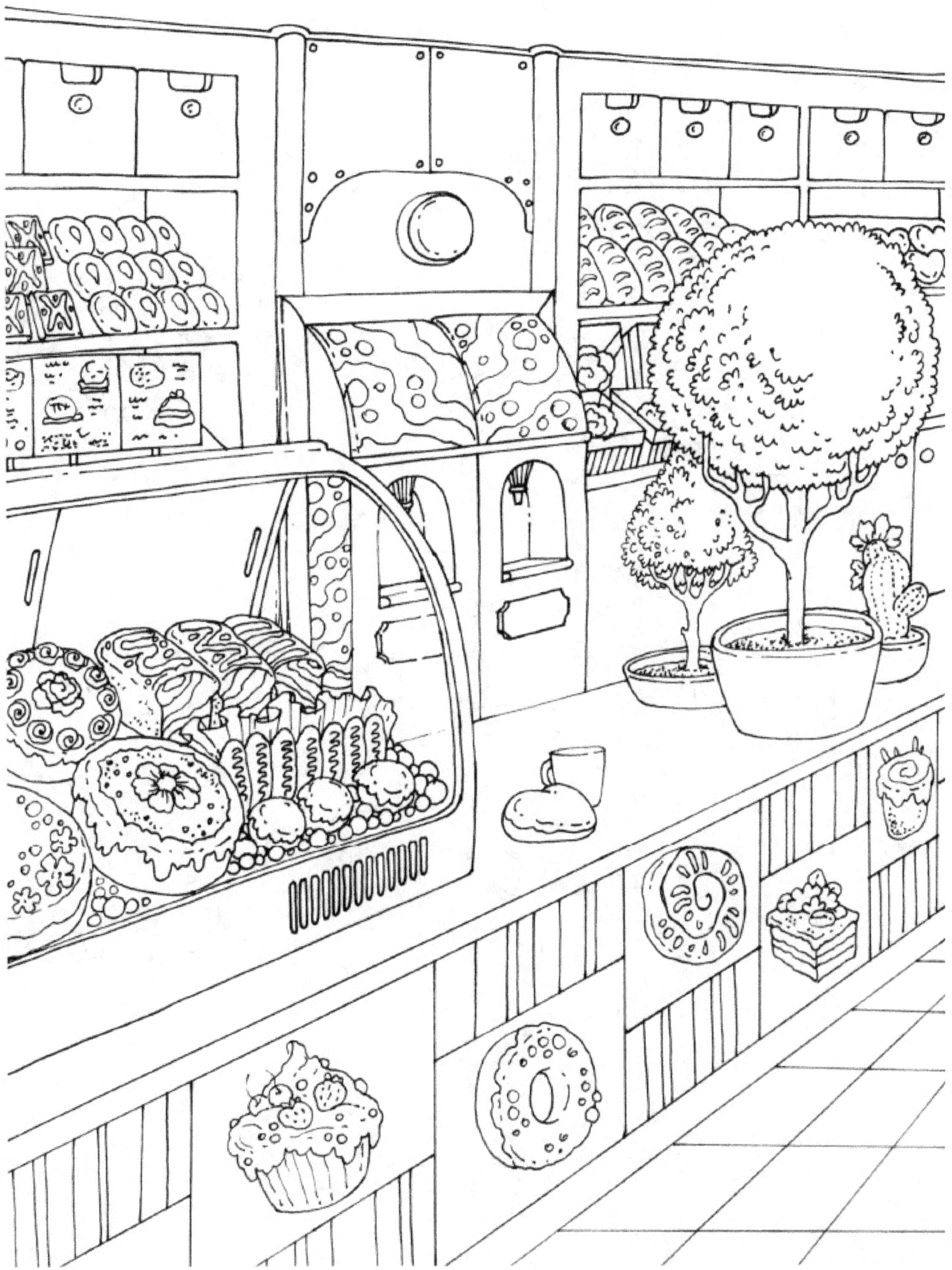

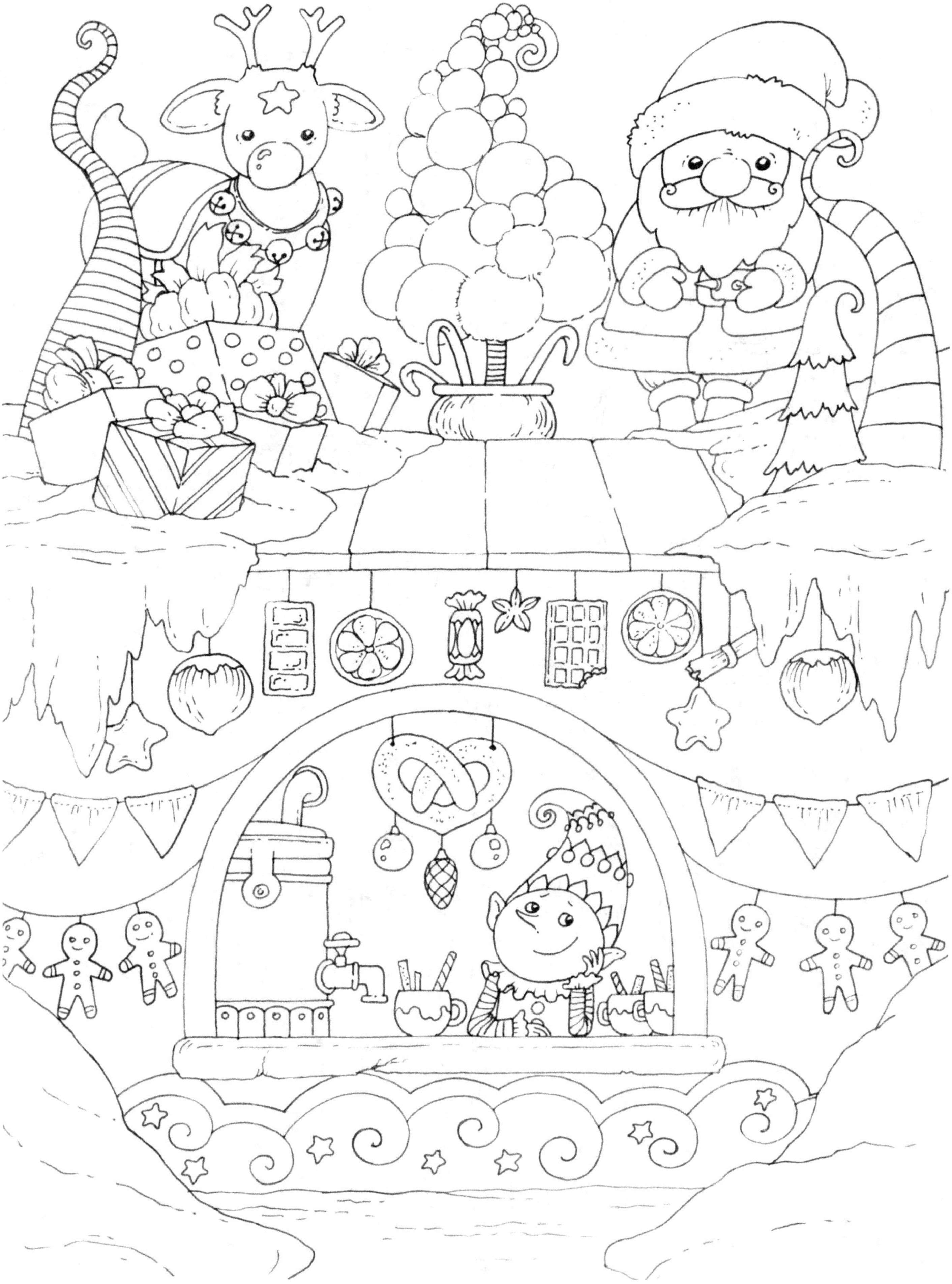

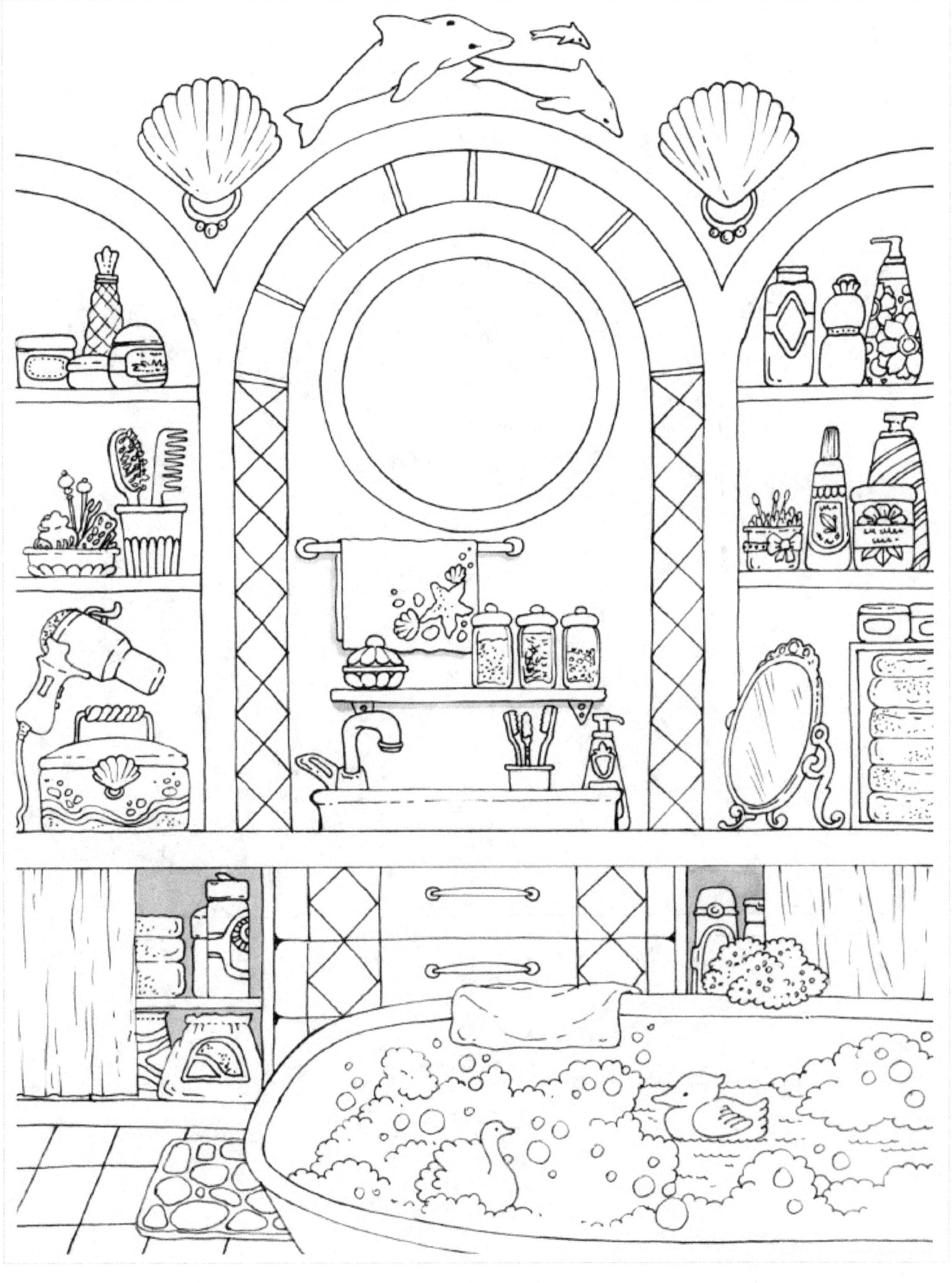

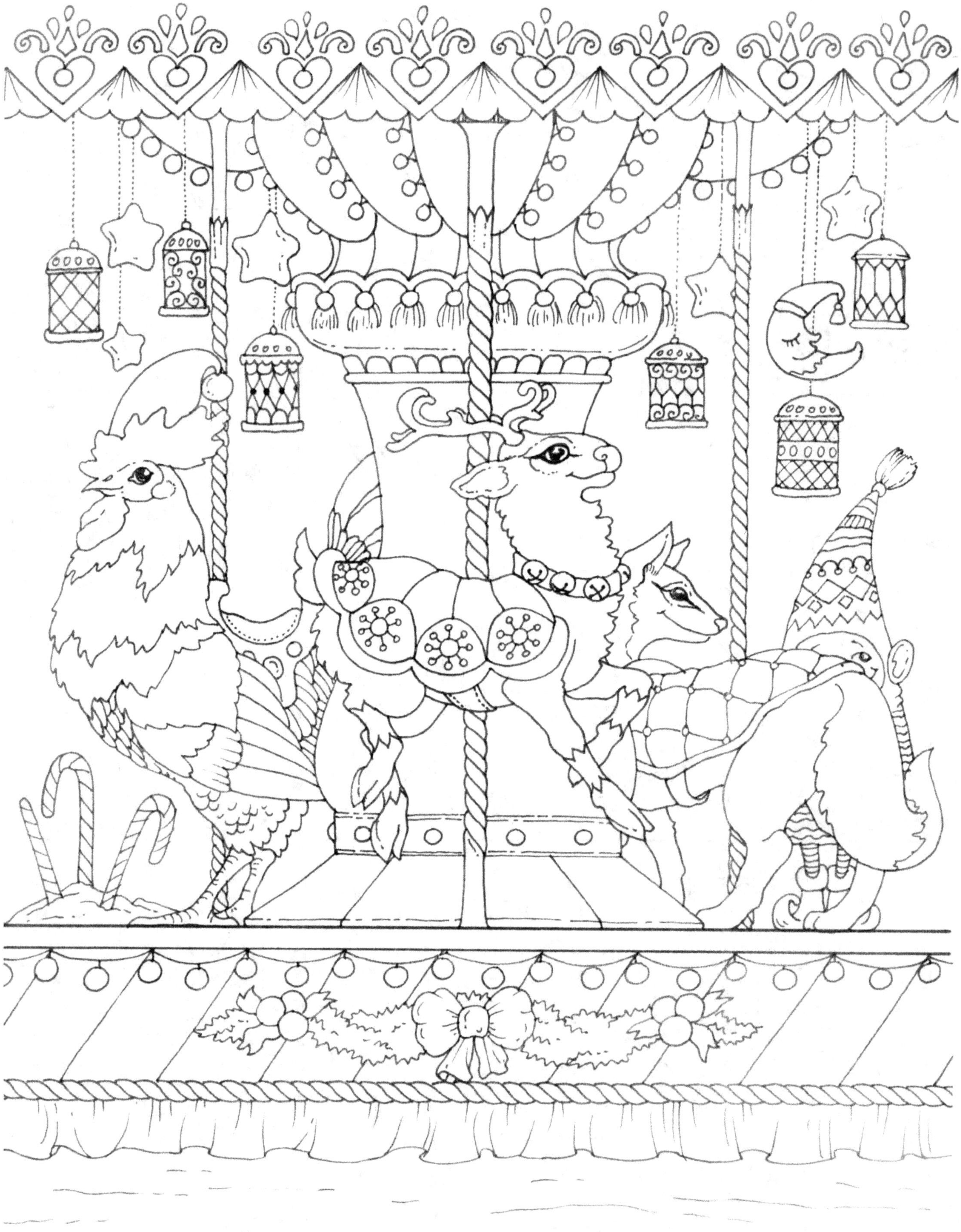

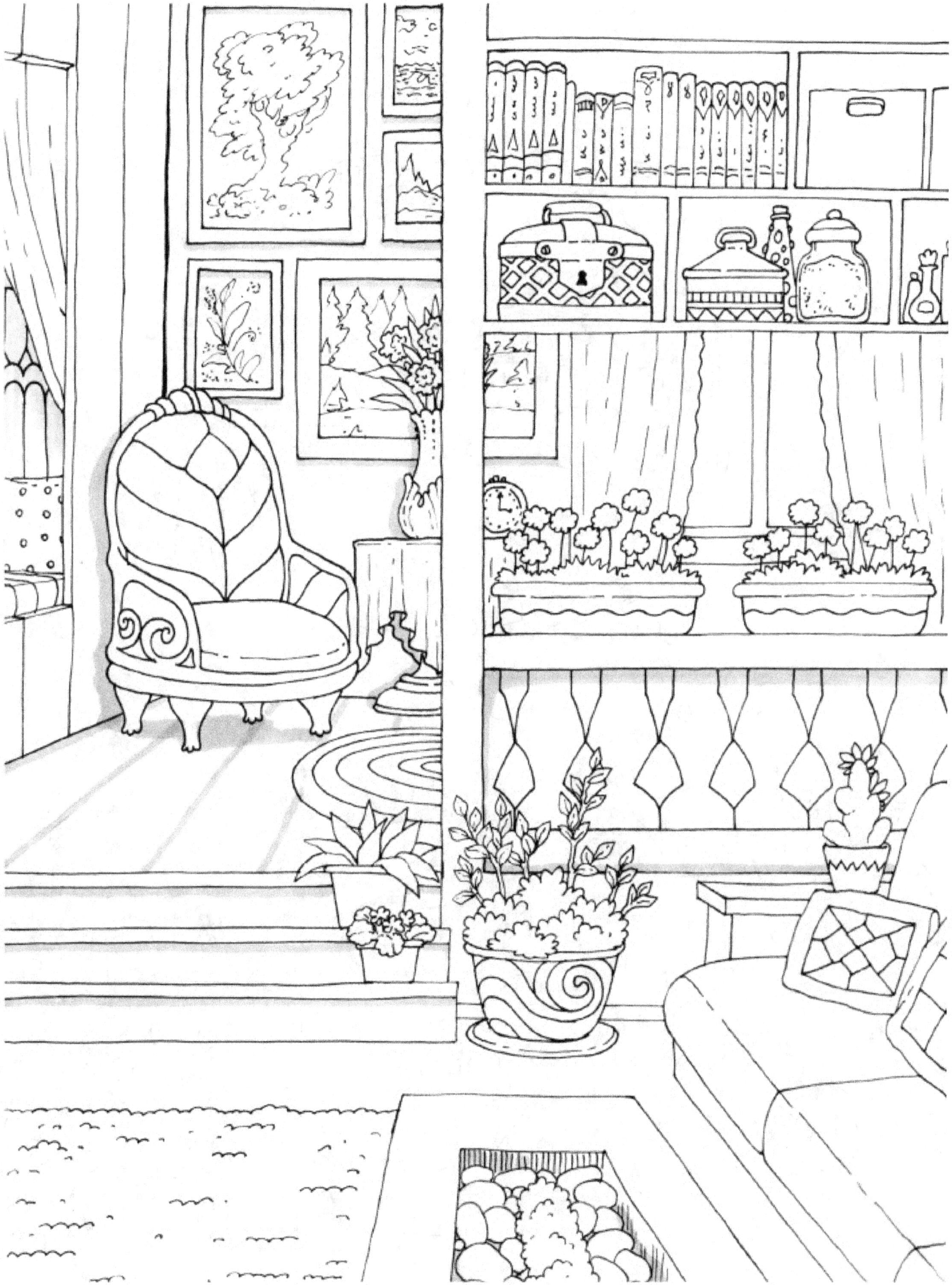

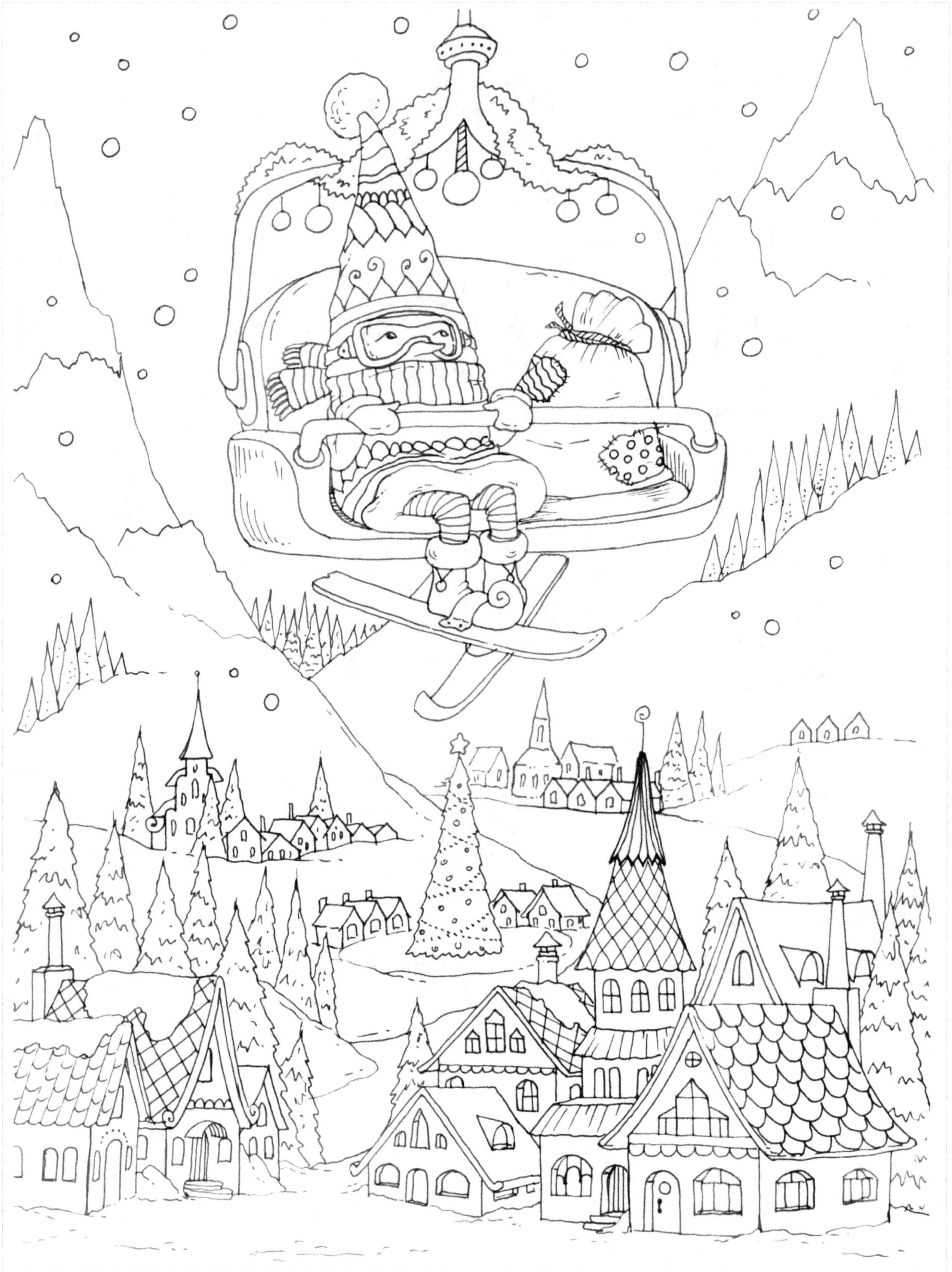

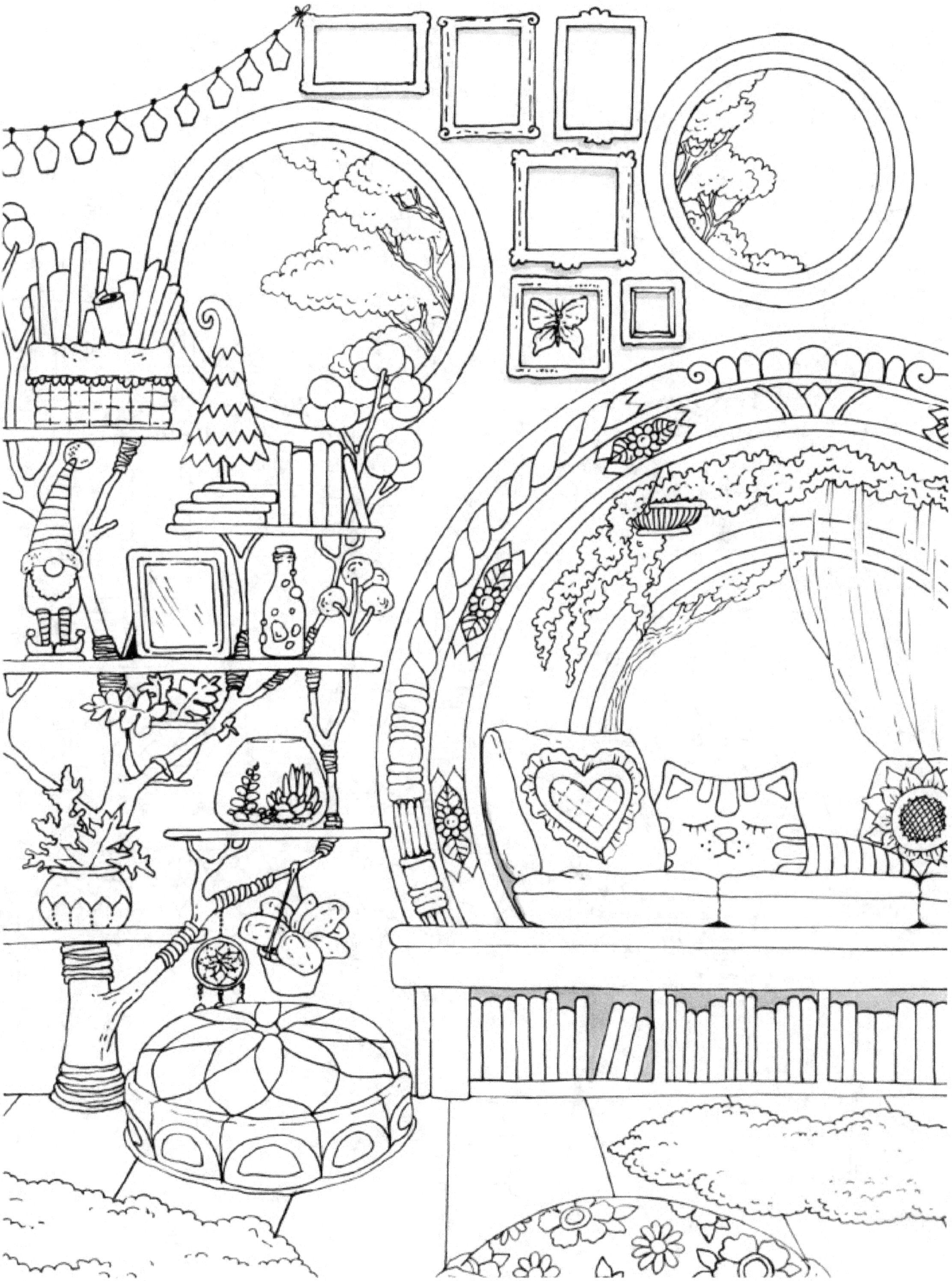

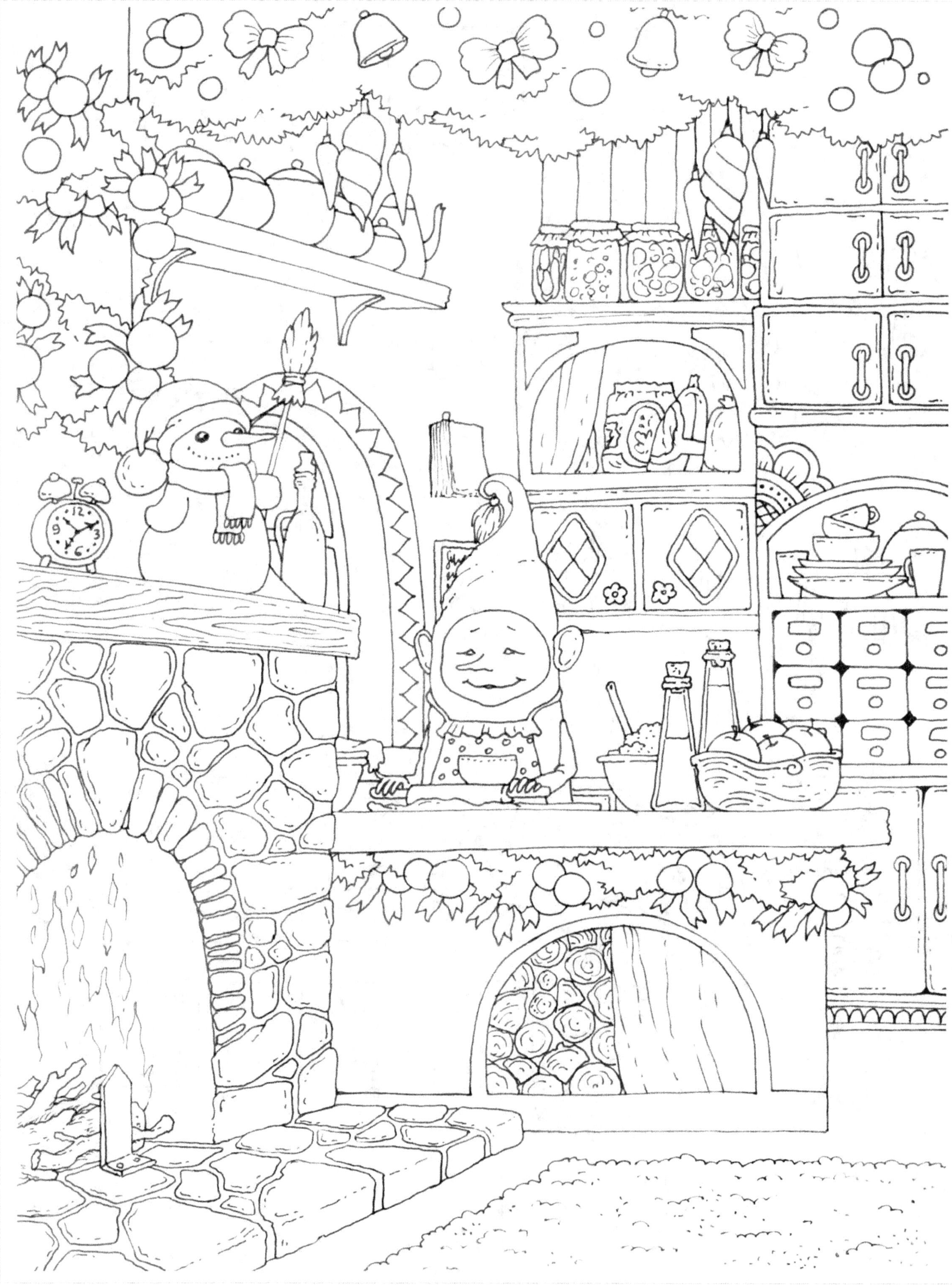

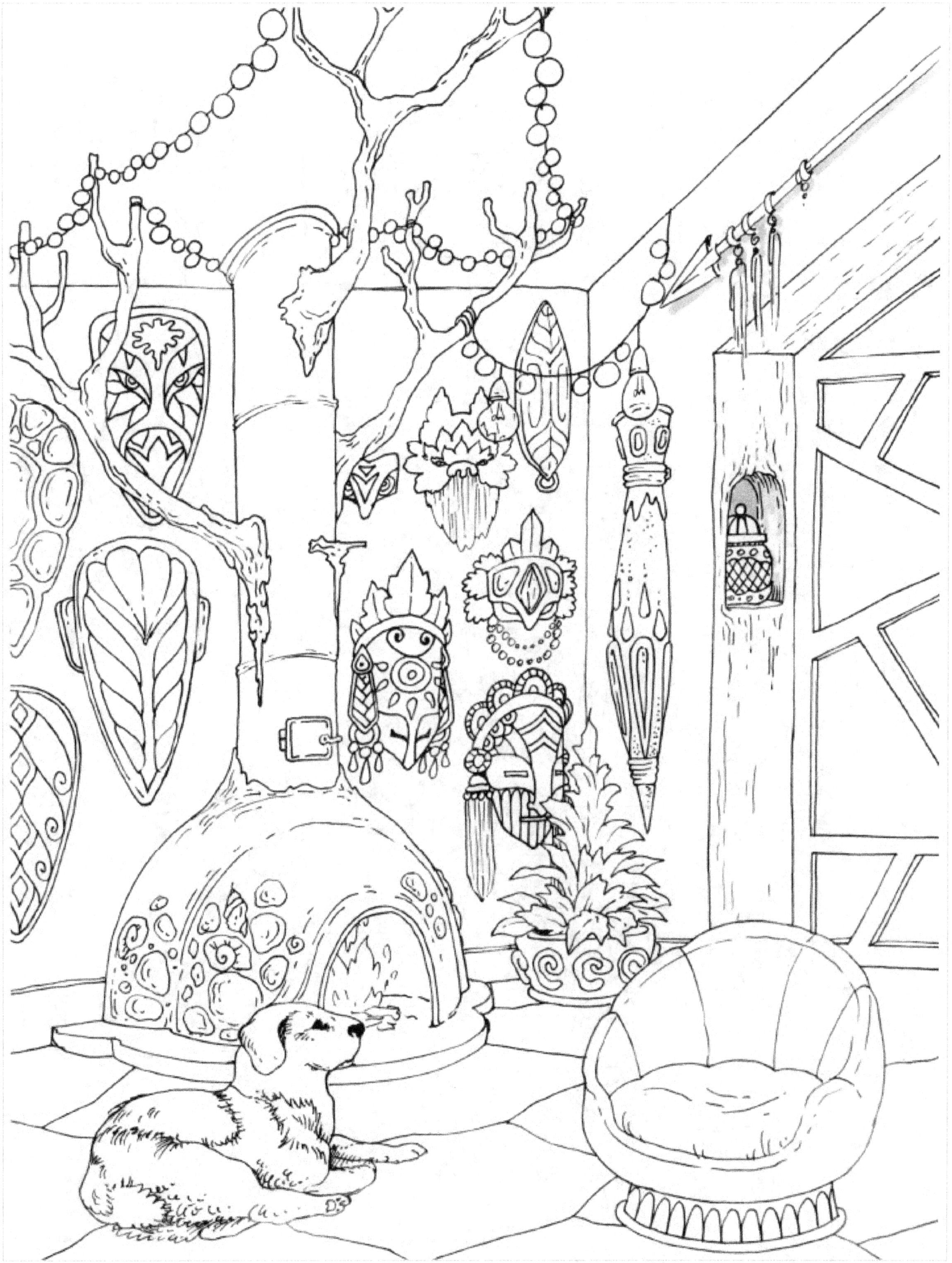

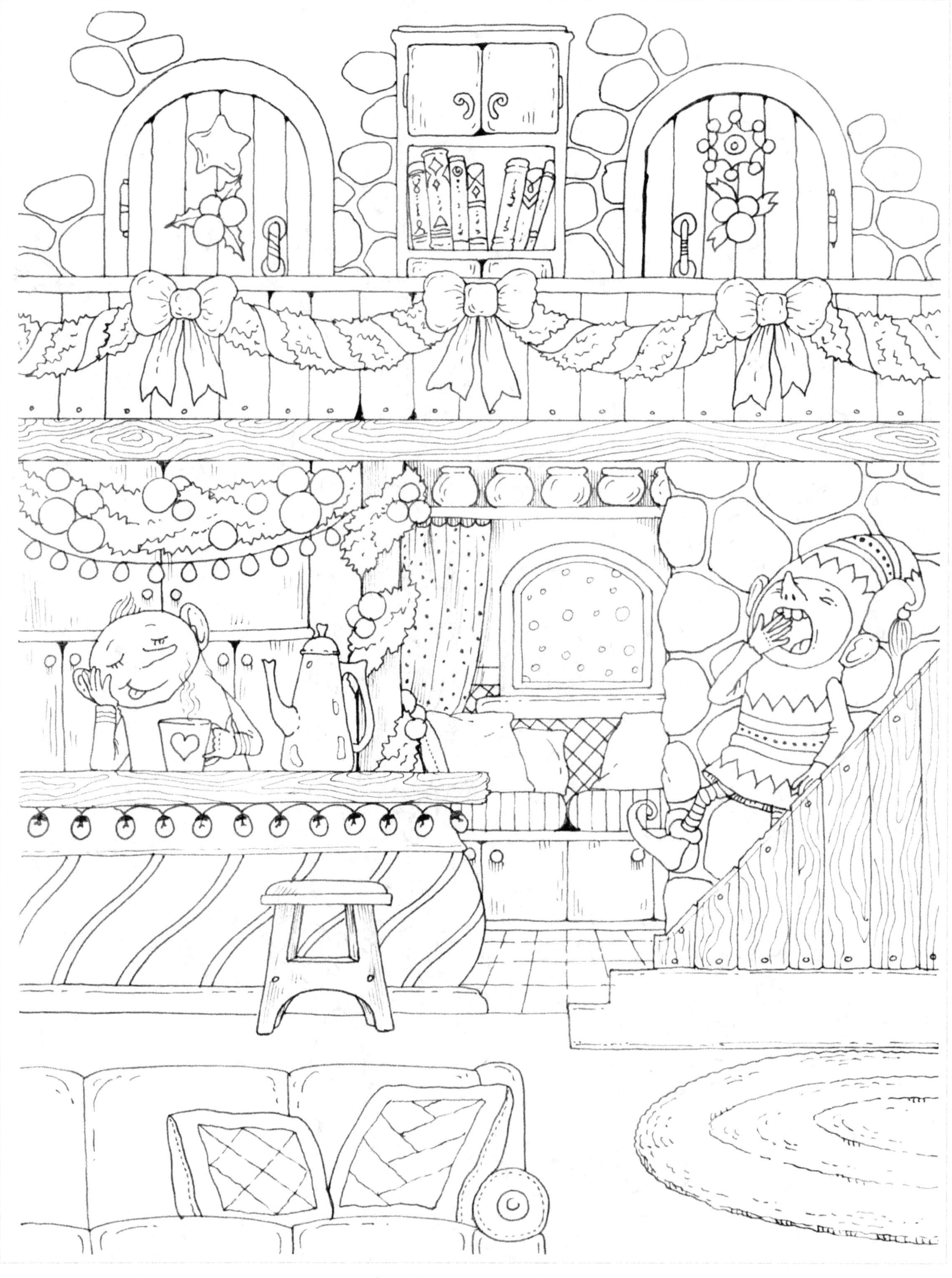

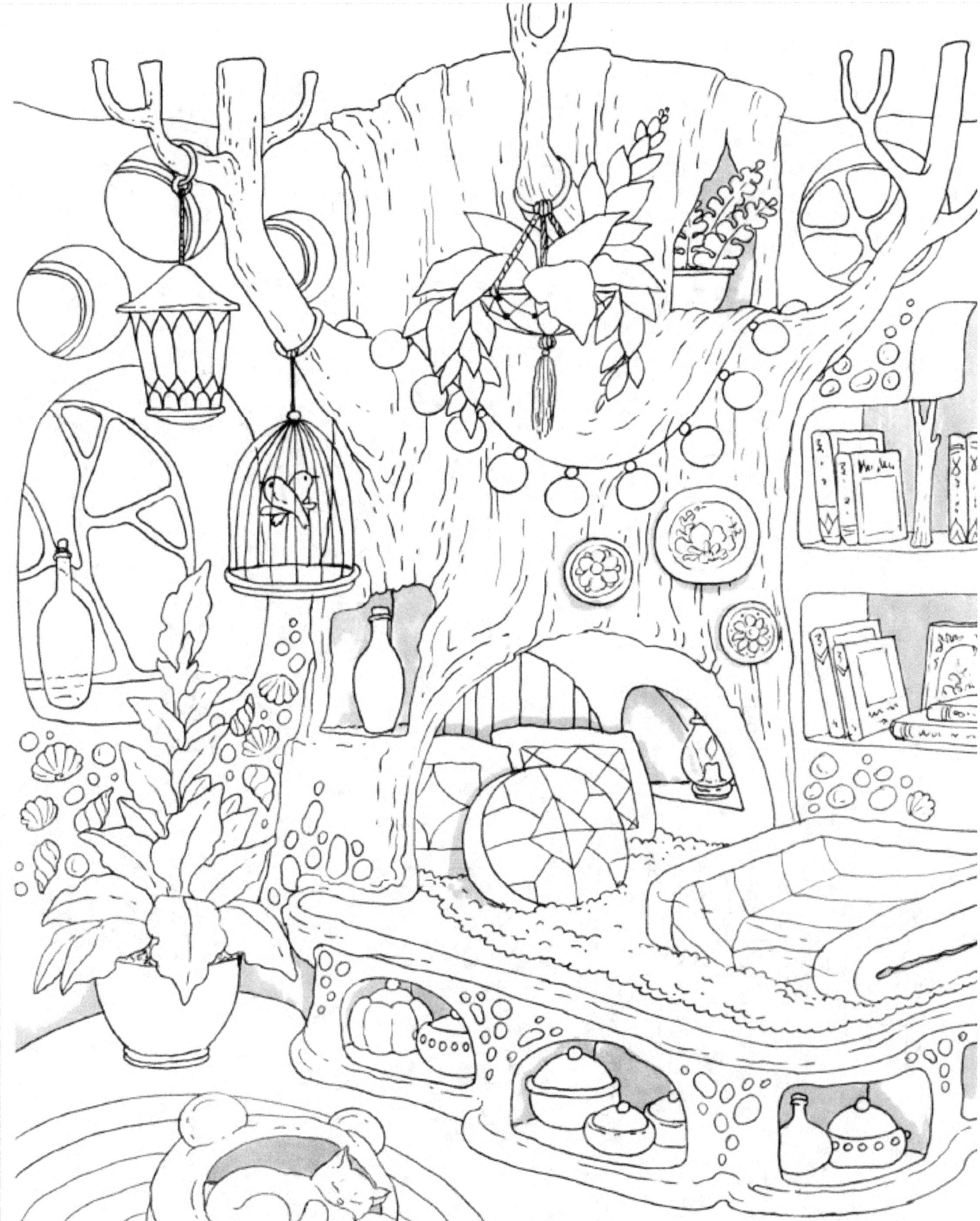

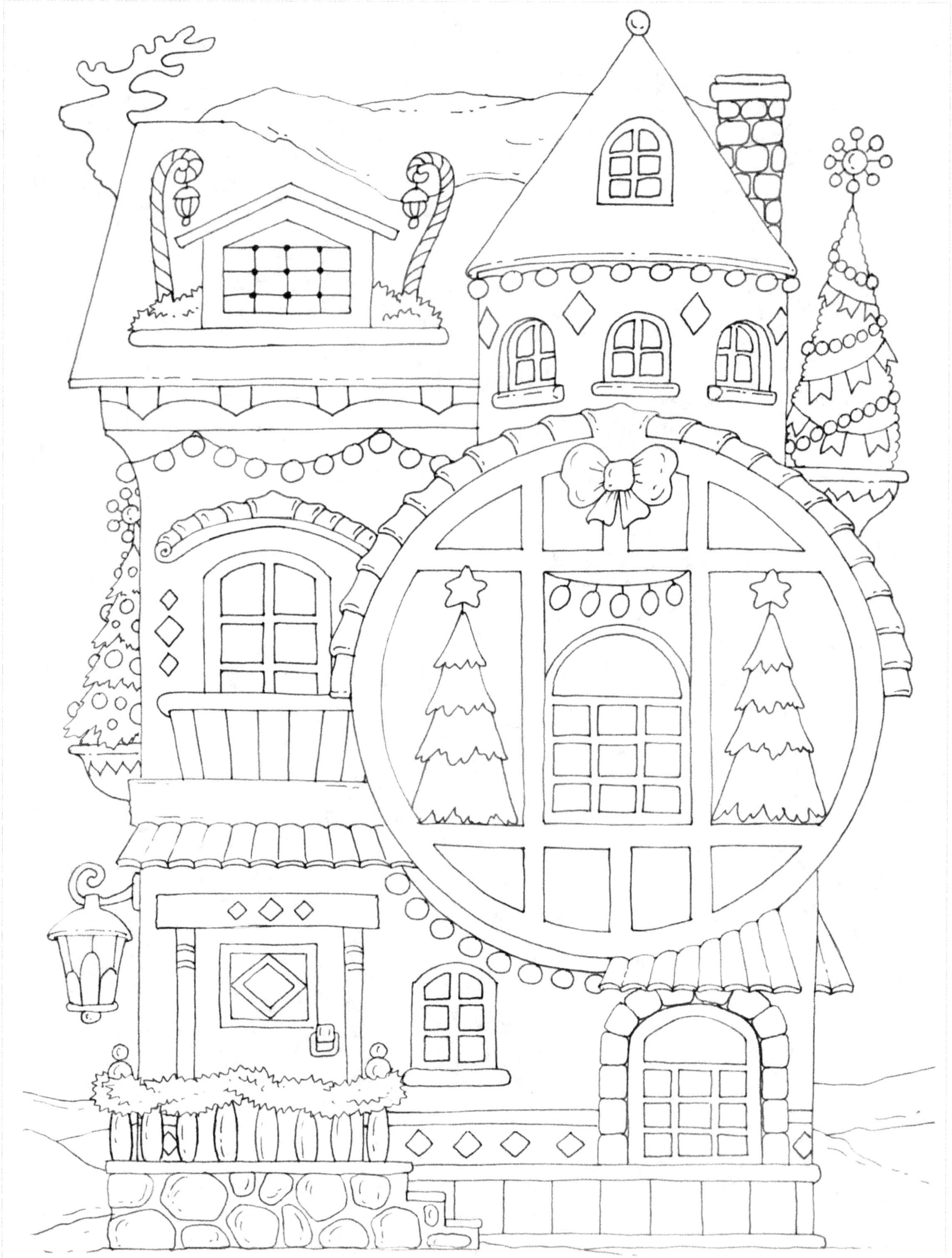

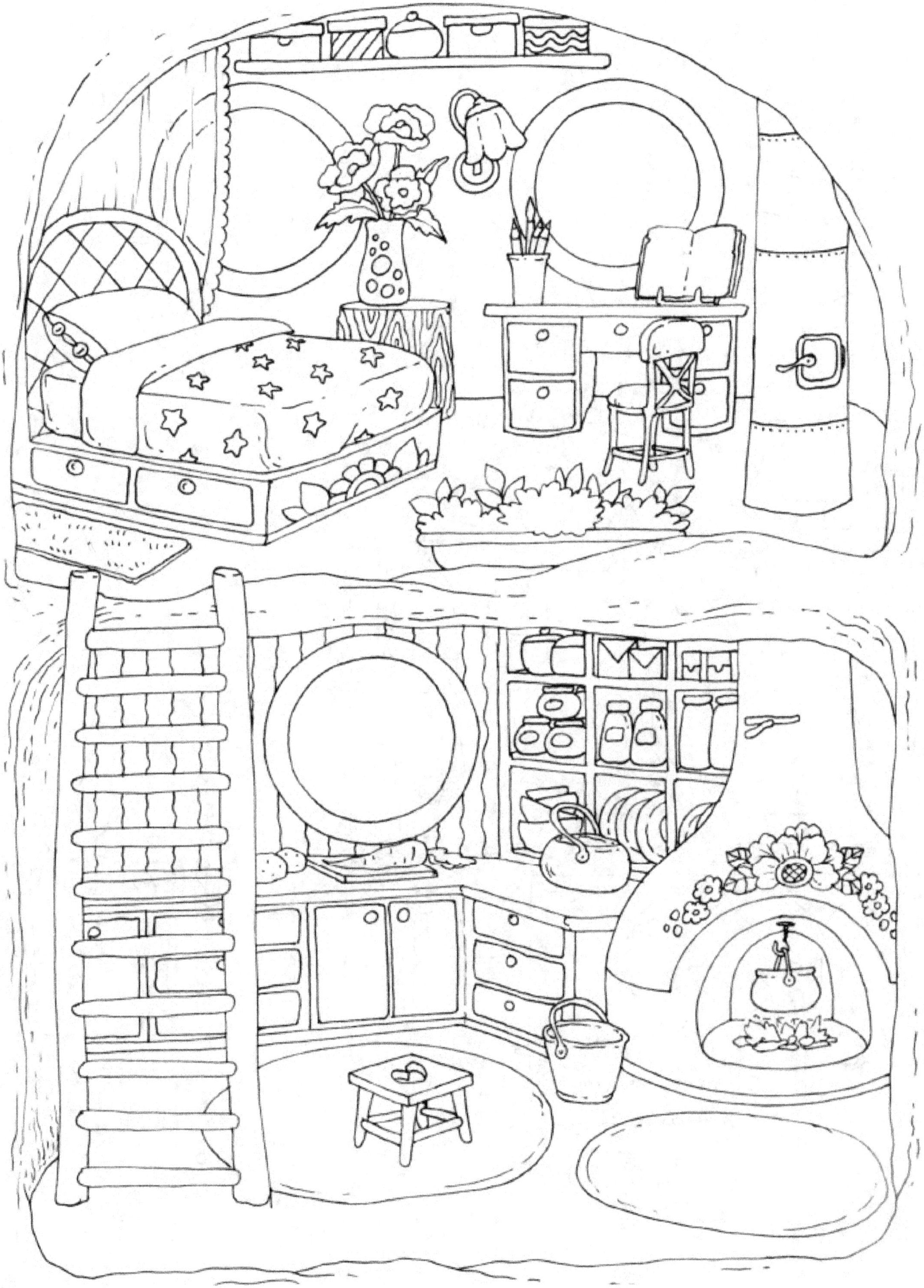

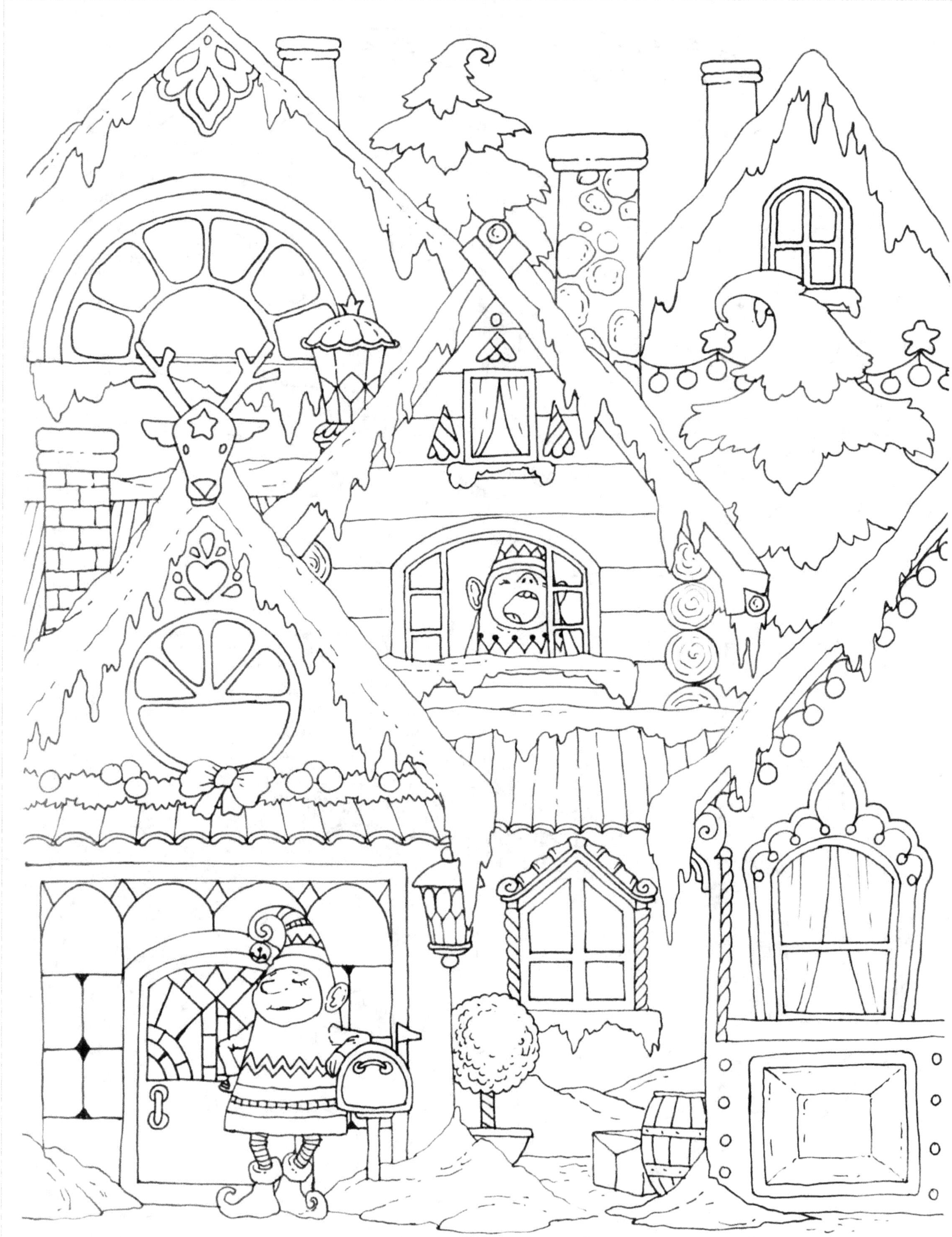

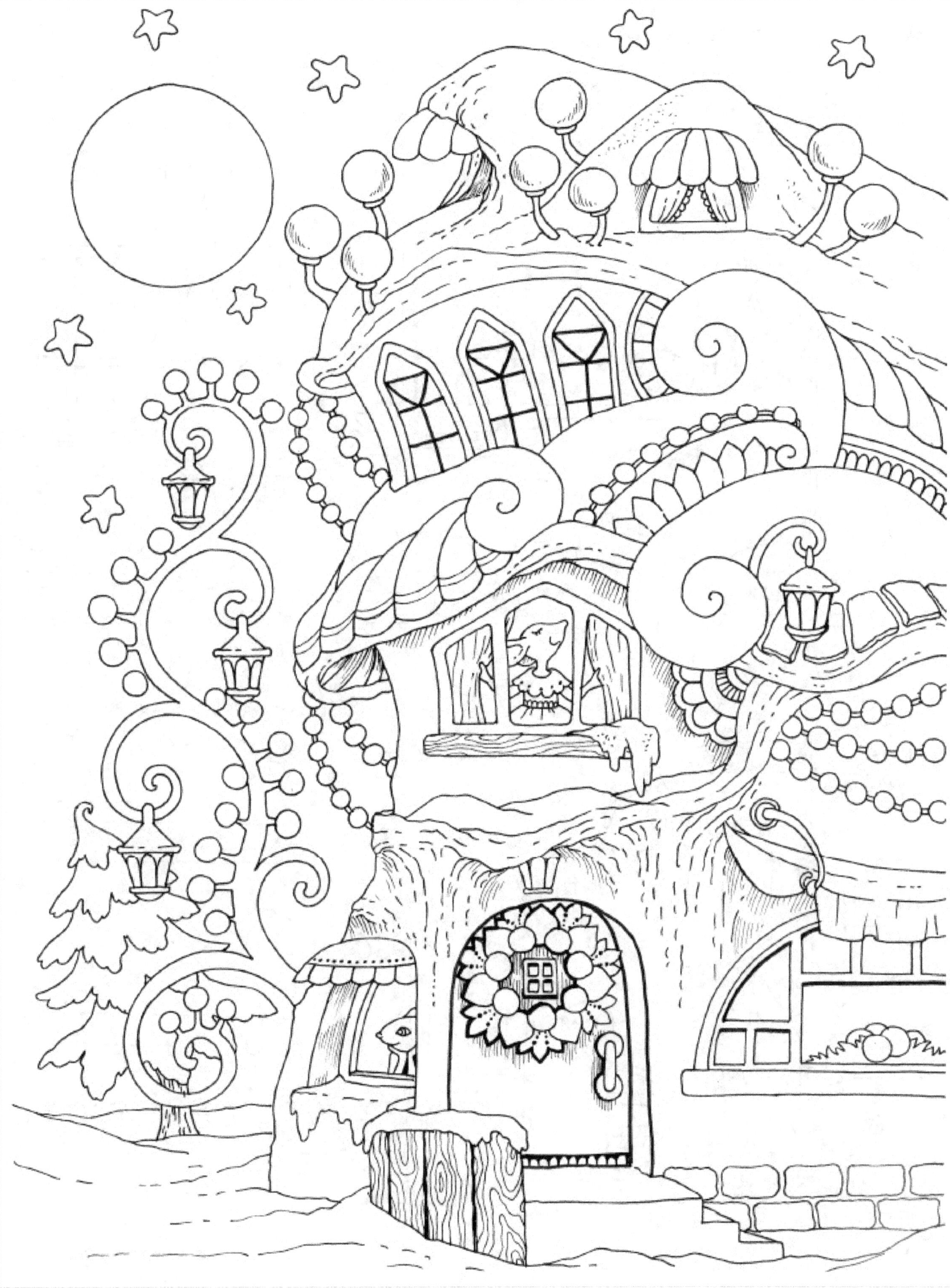

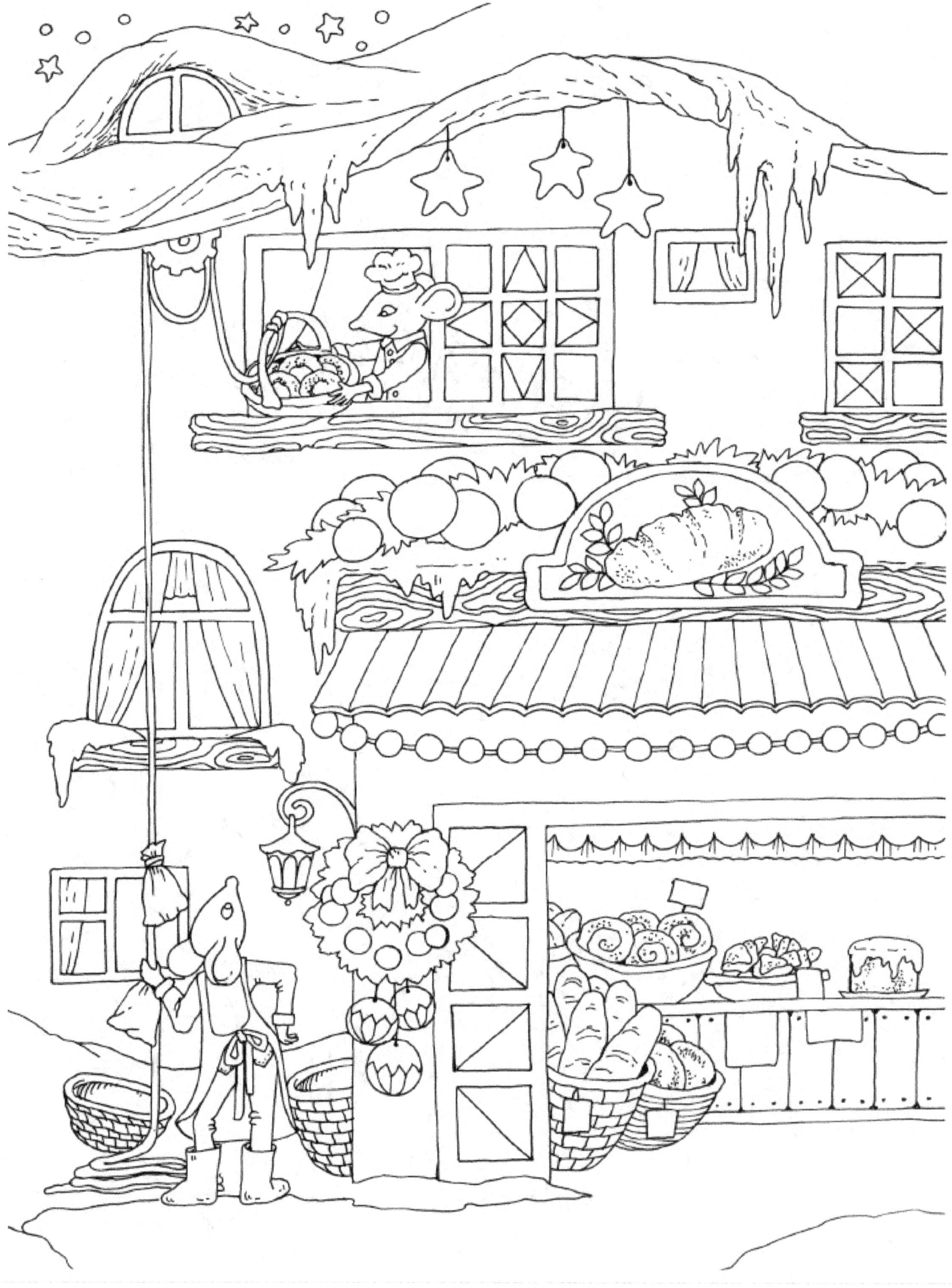

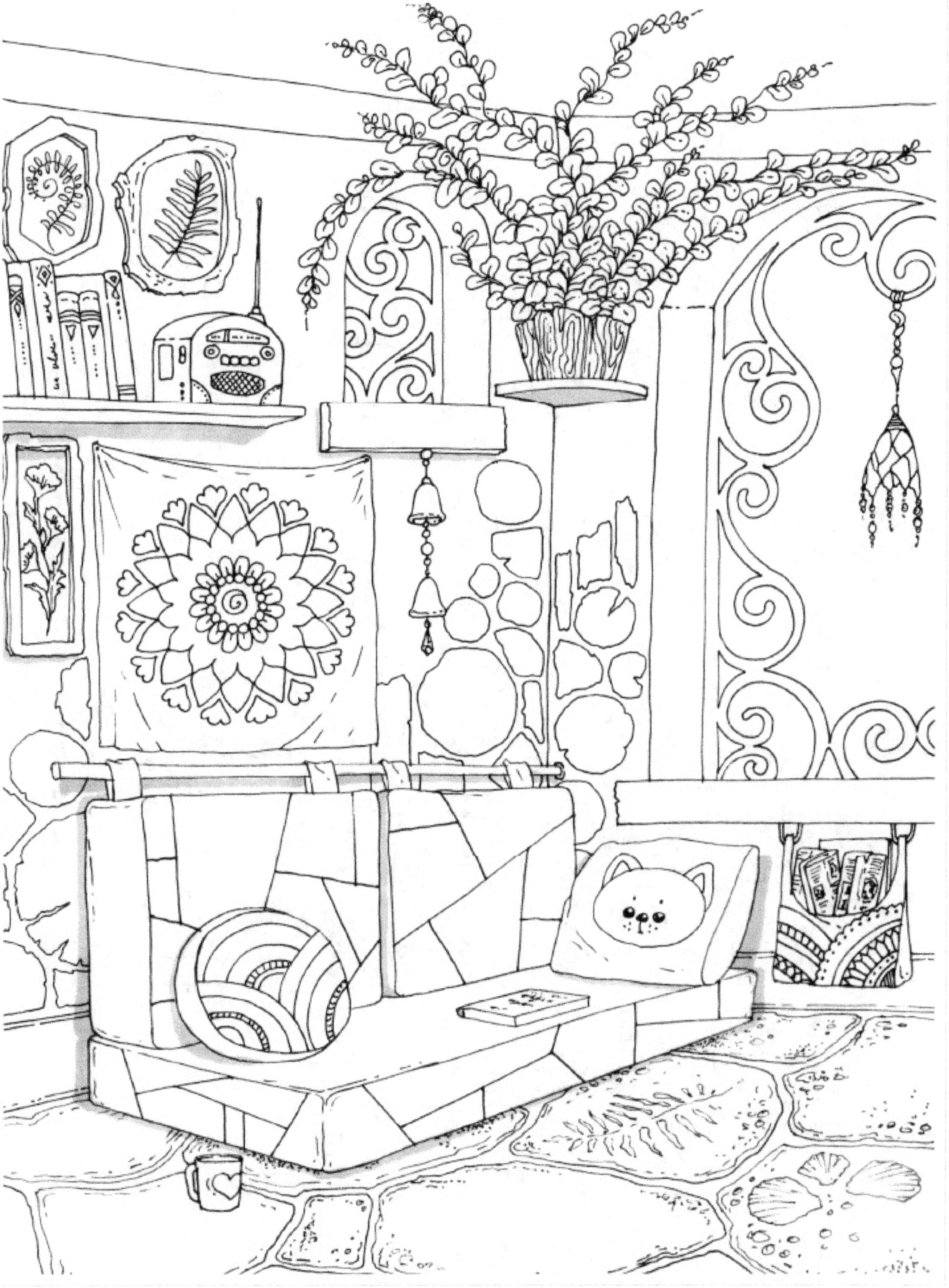

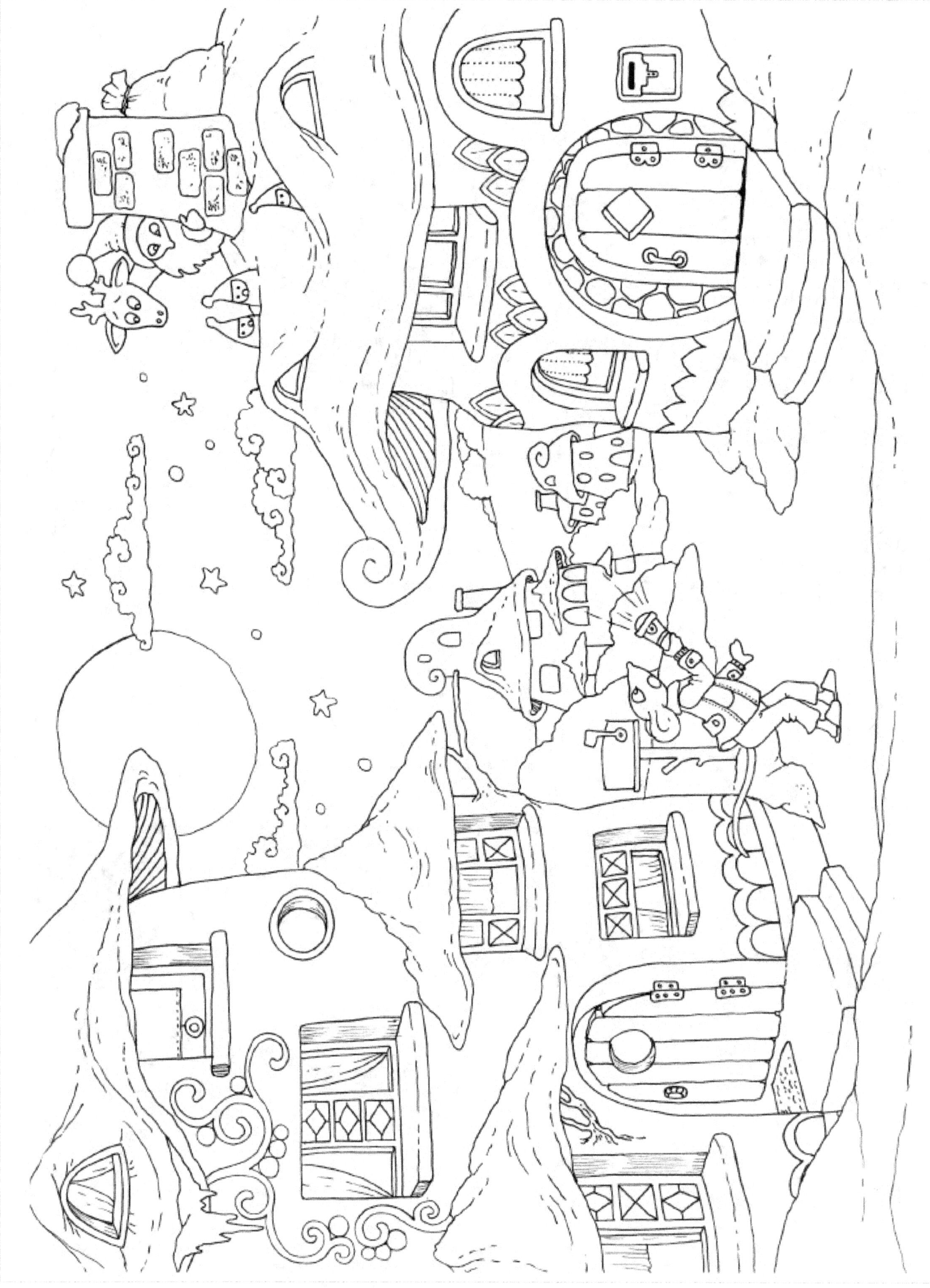

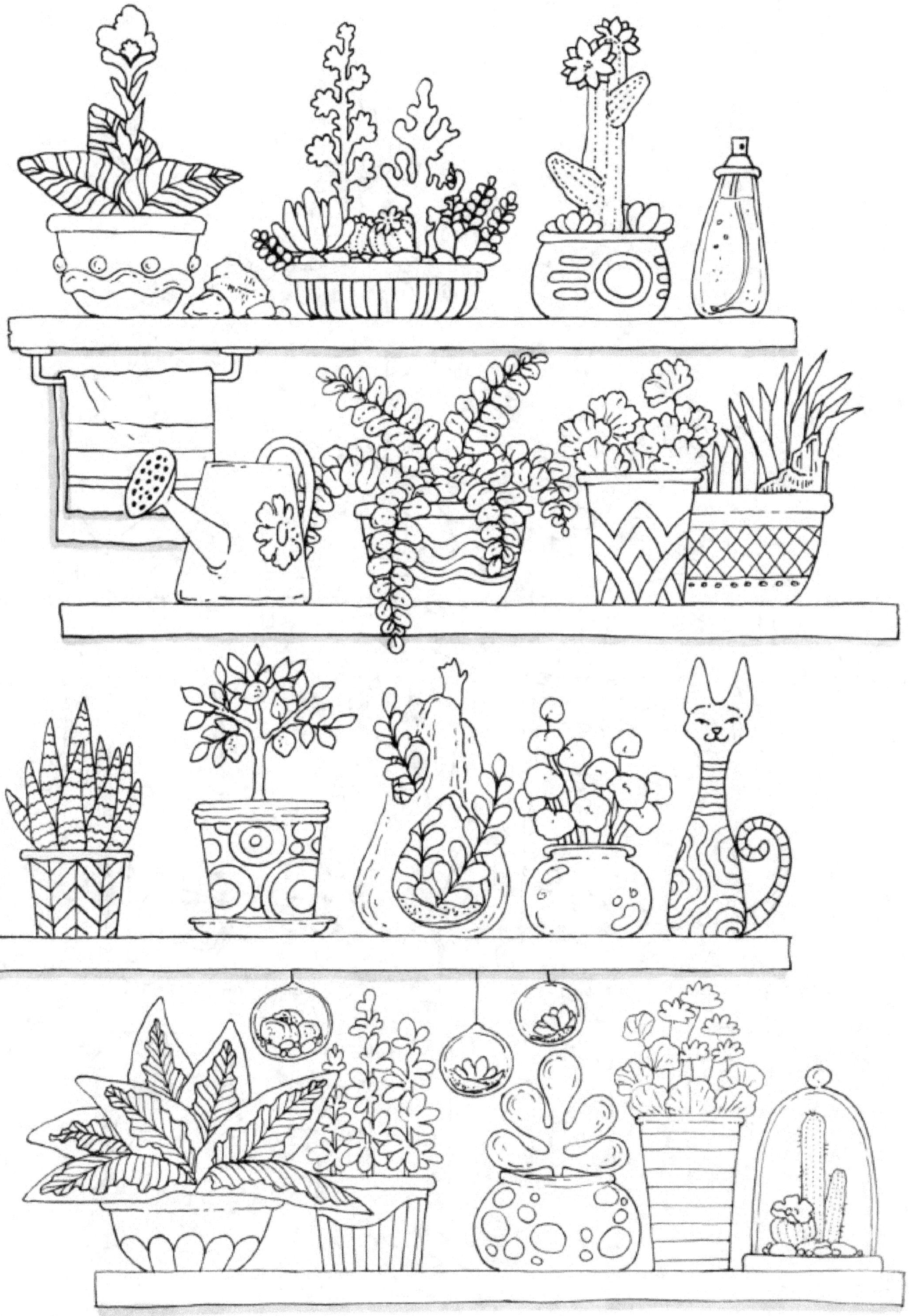

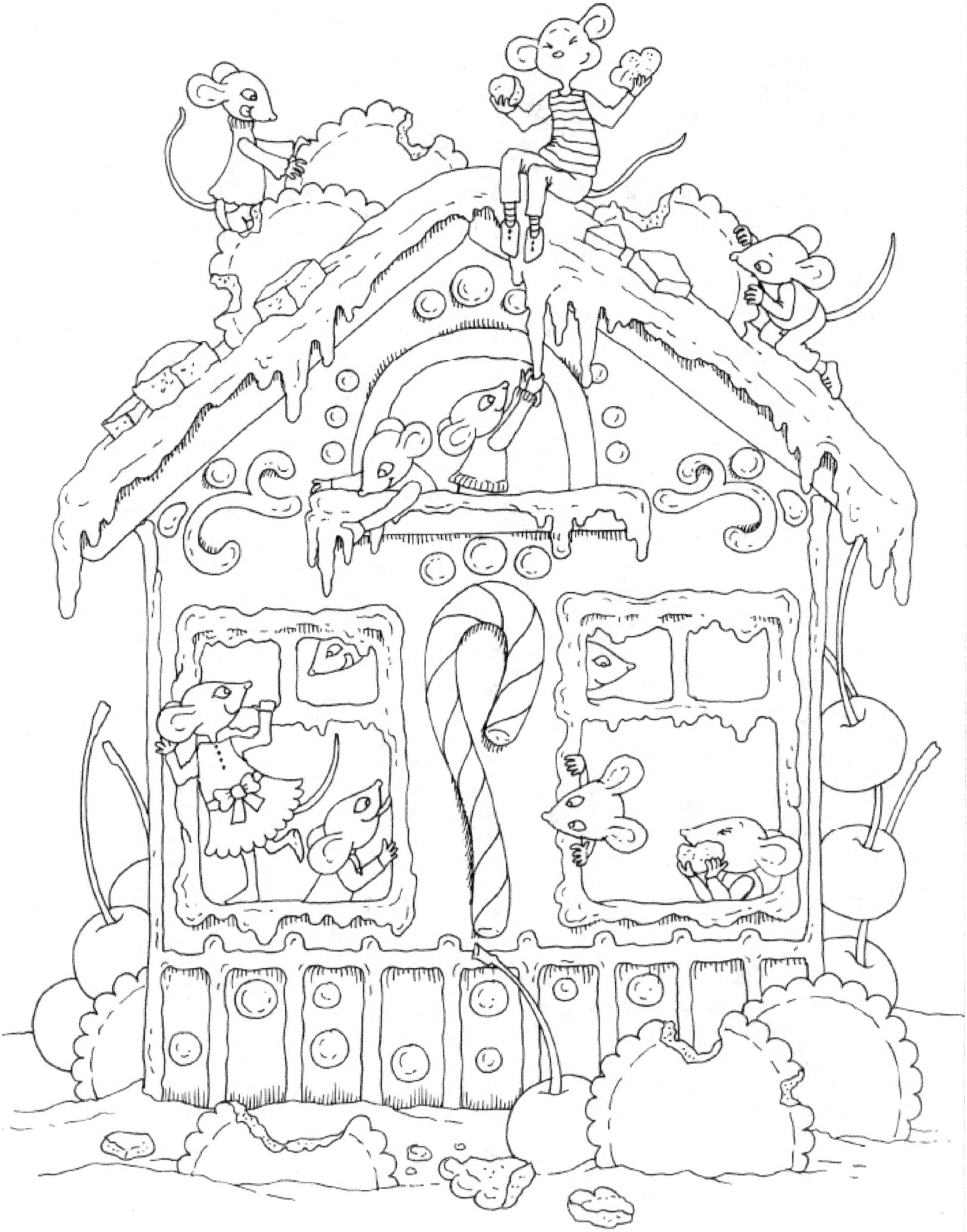

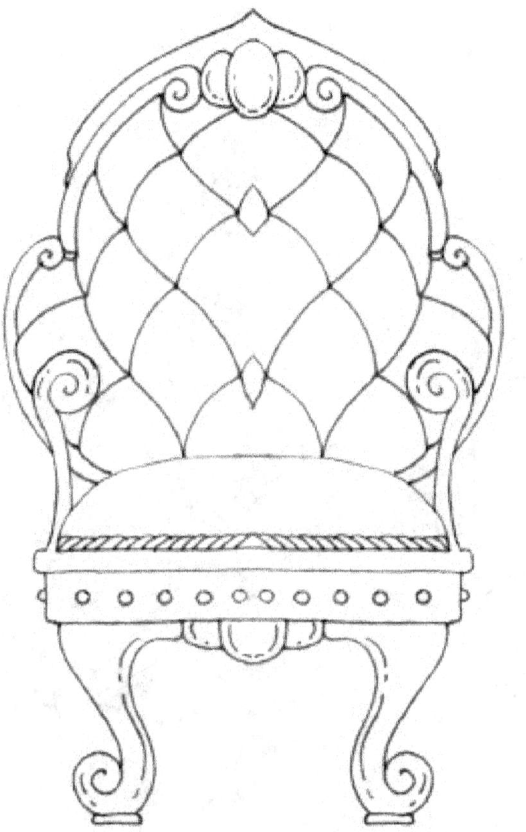
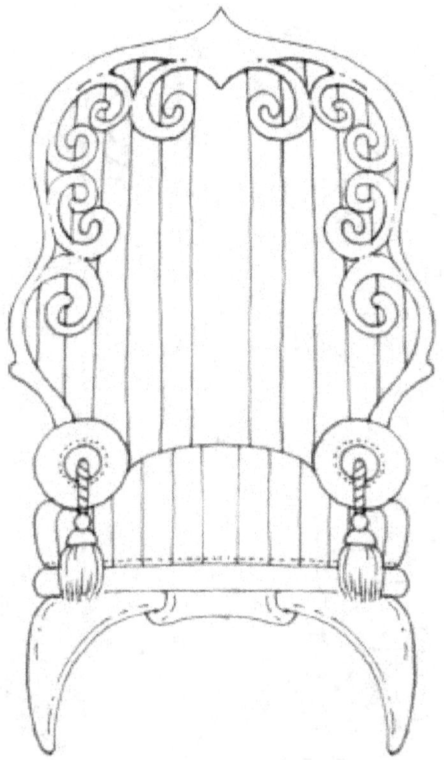
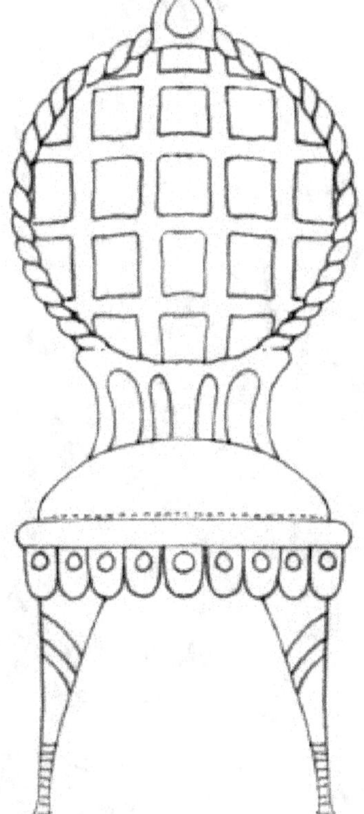
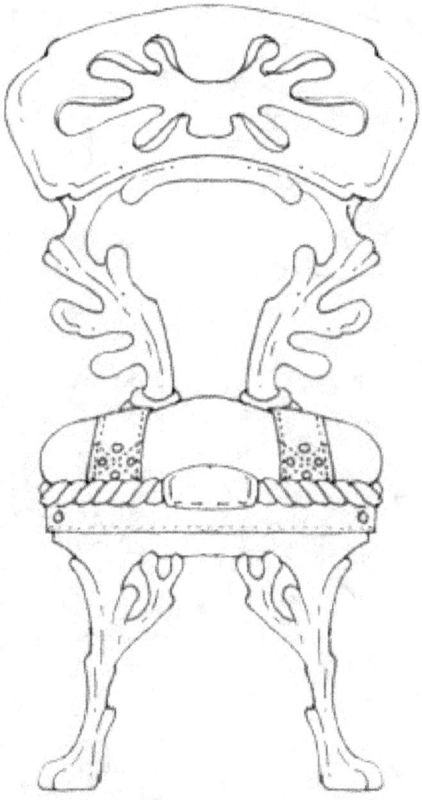
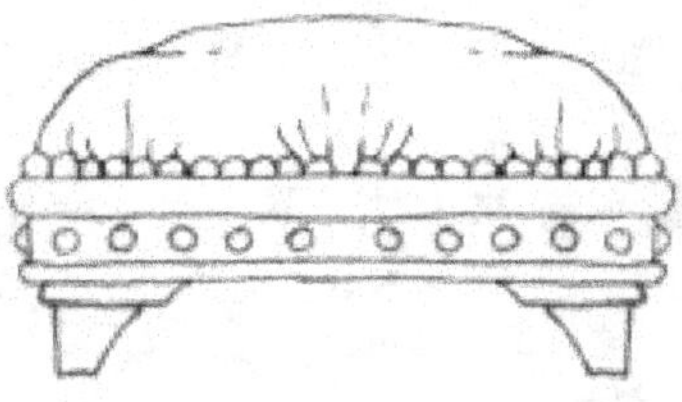

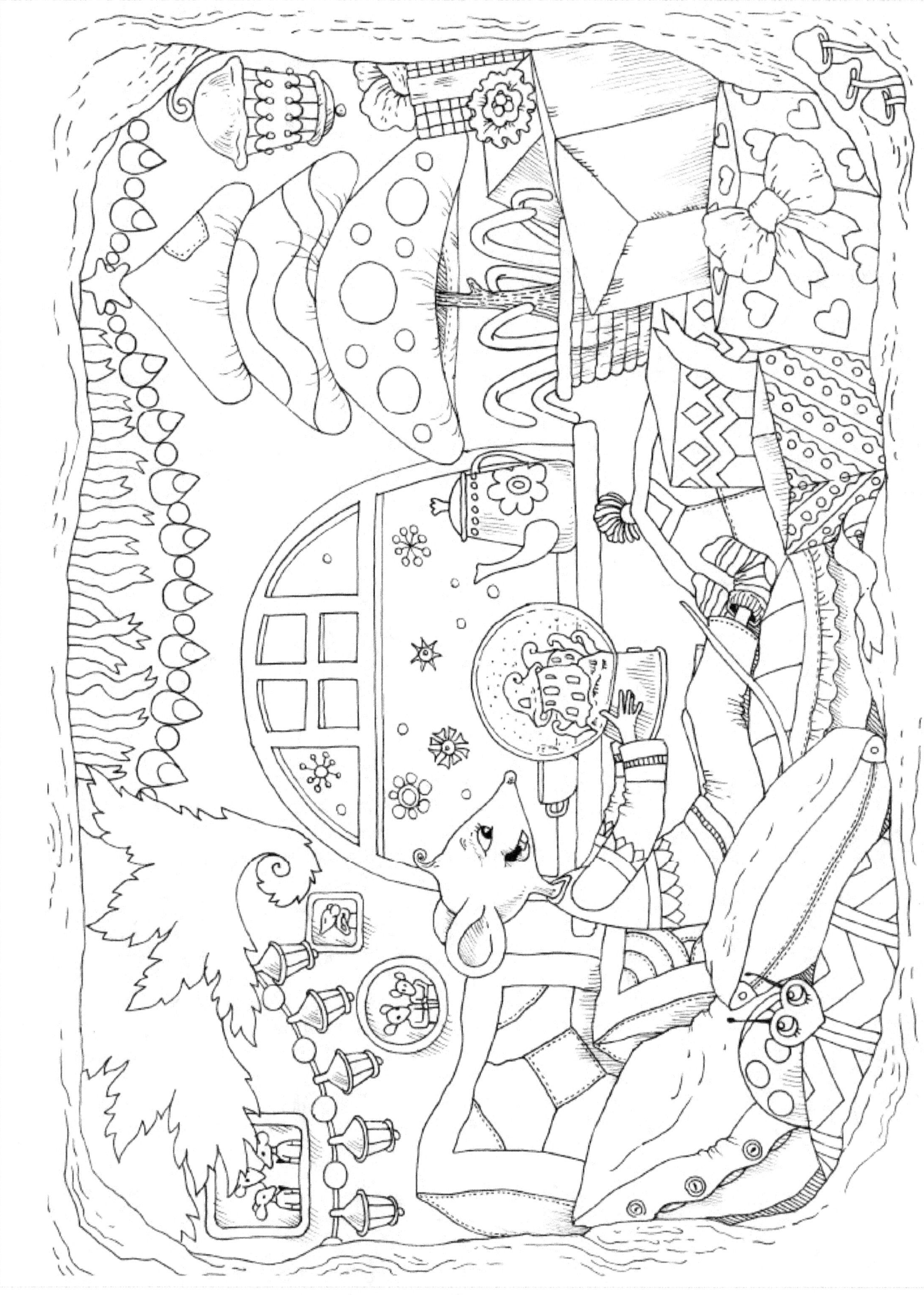

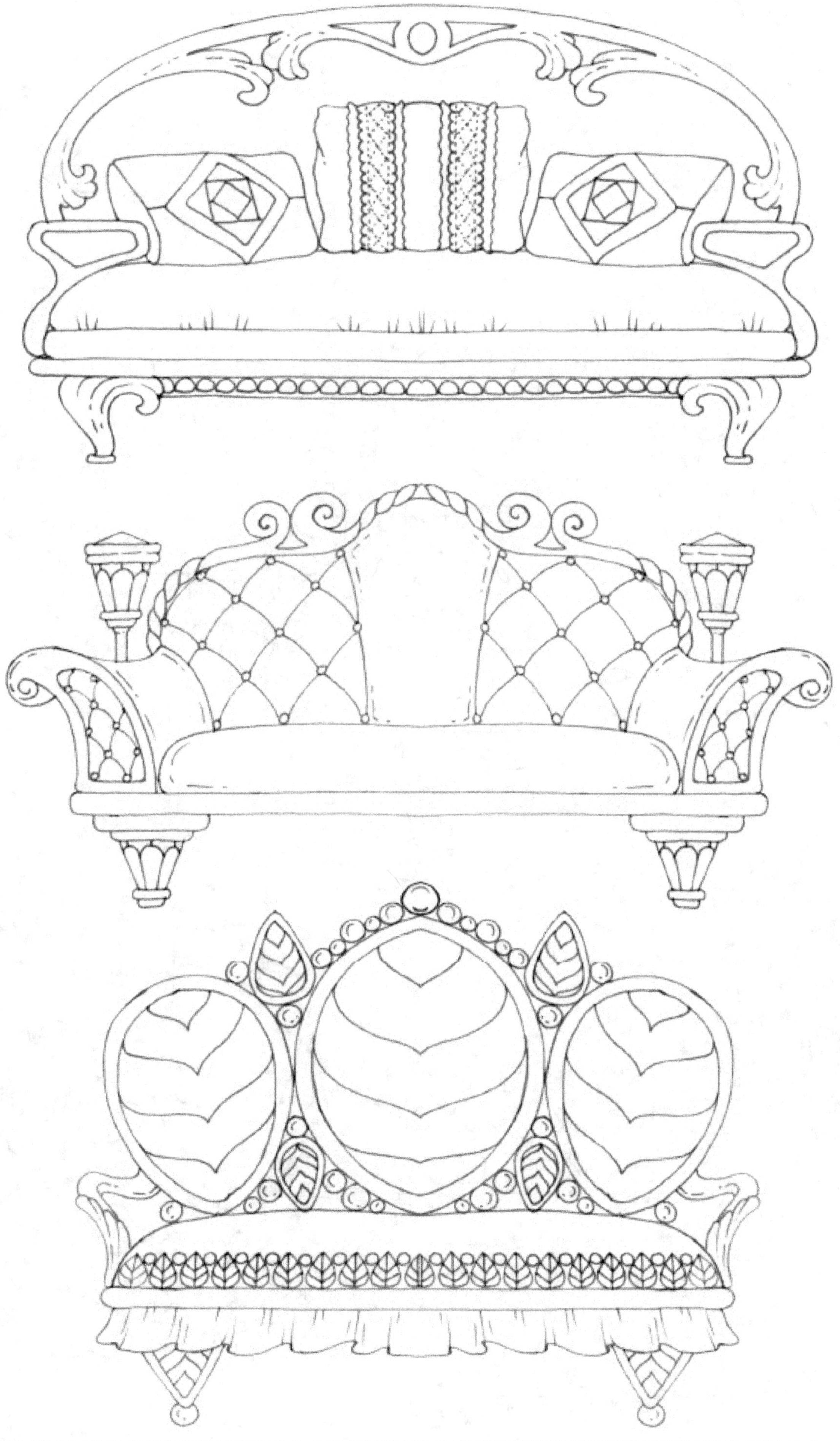

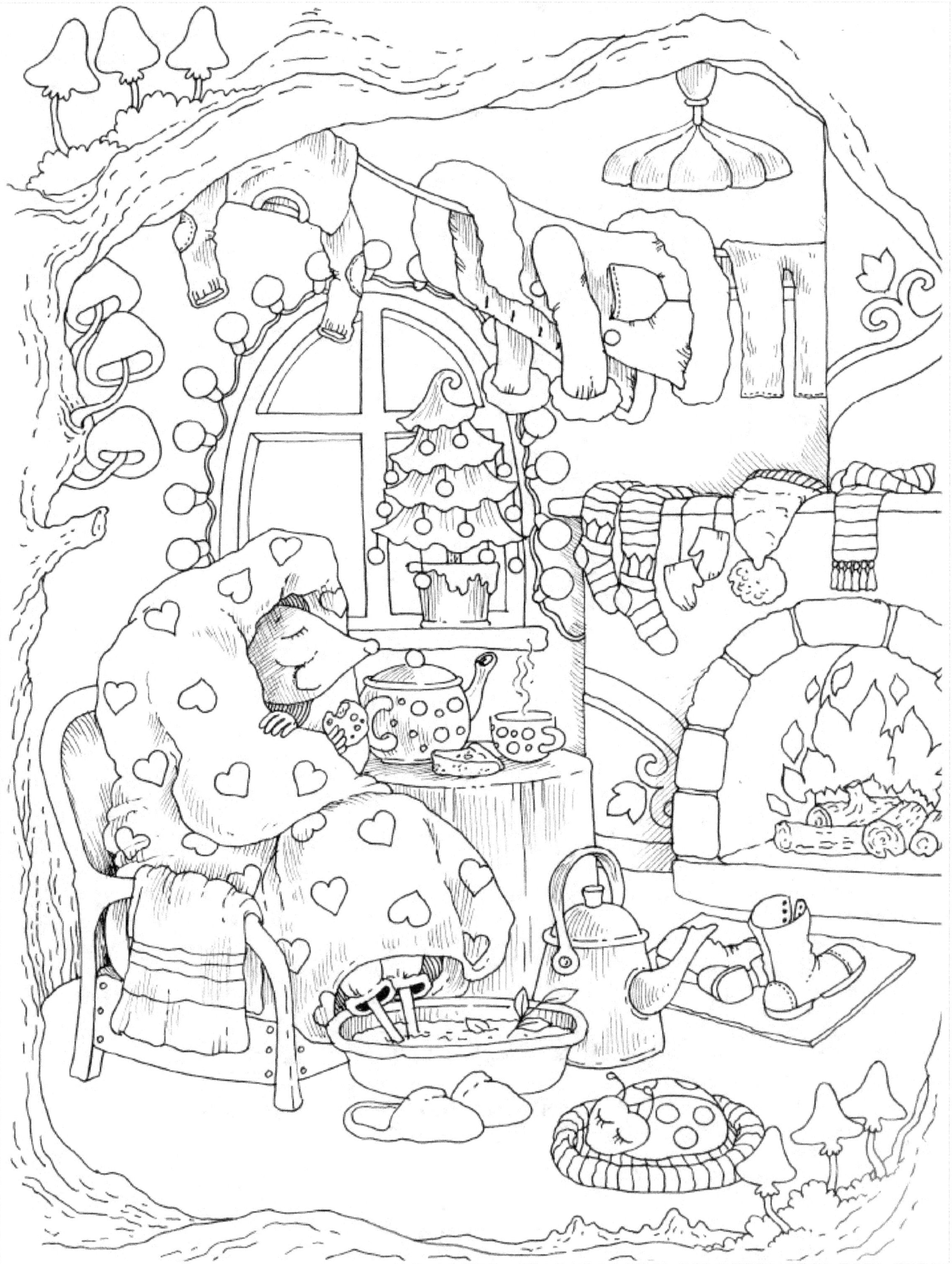

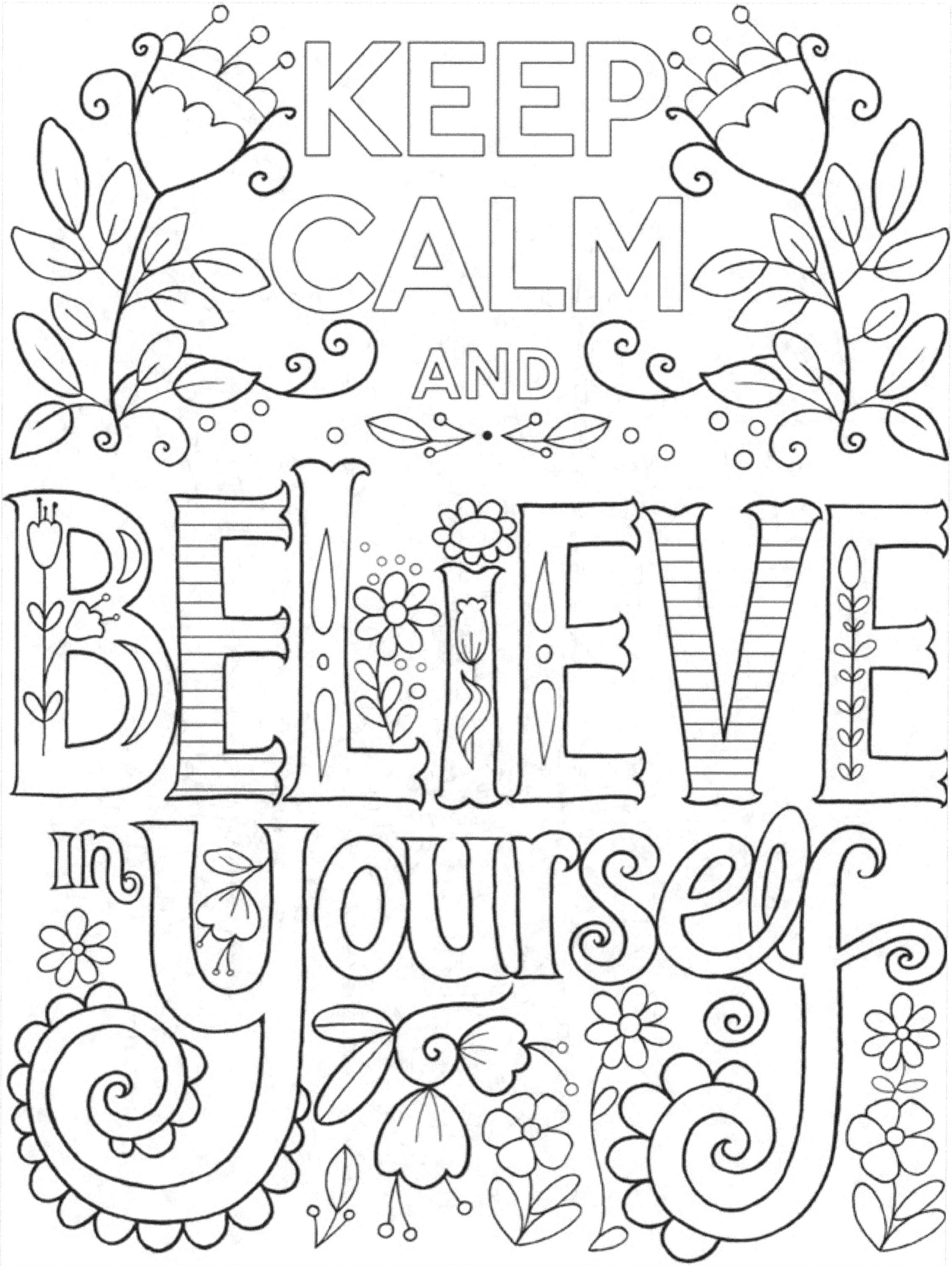
KEEP
CALM
AND
BELIEVE
in Yourself

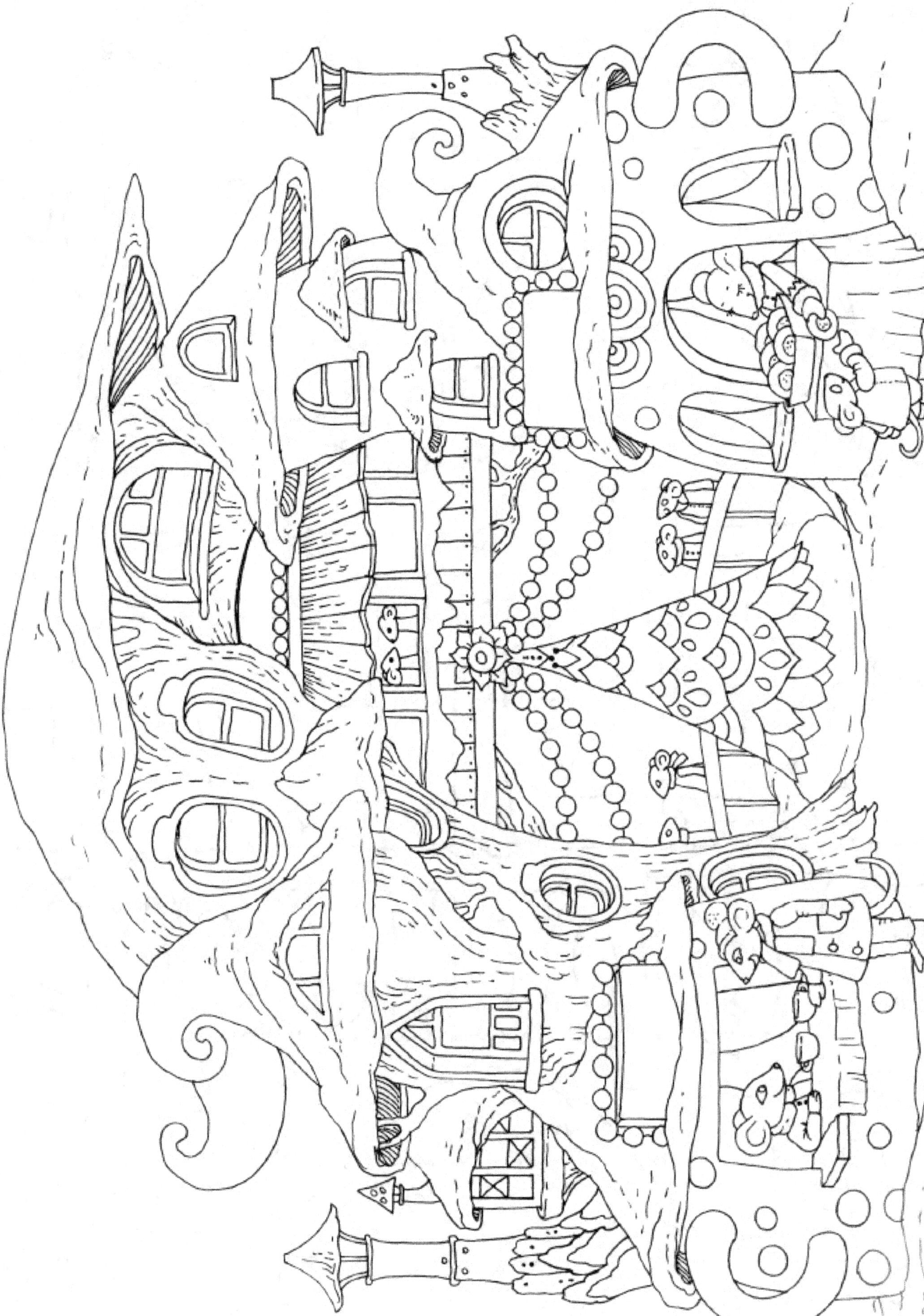

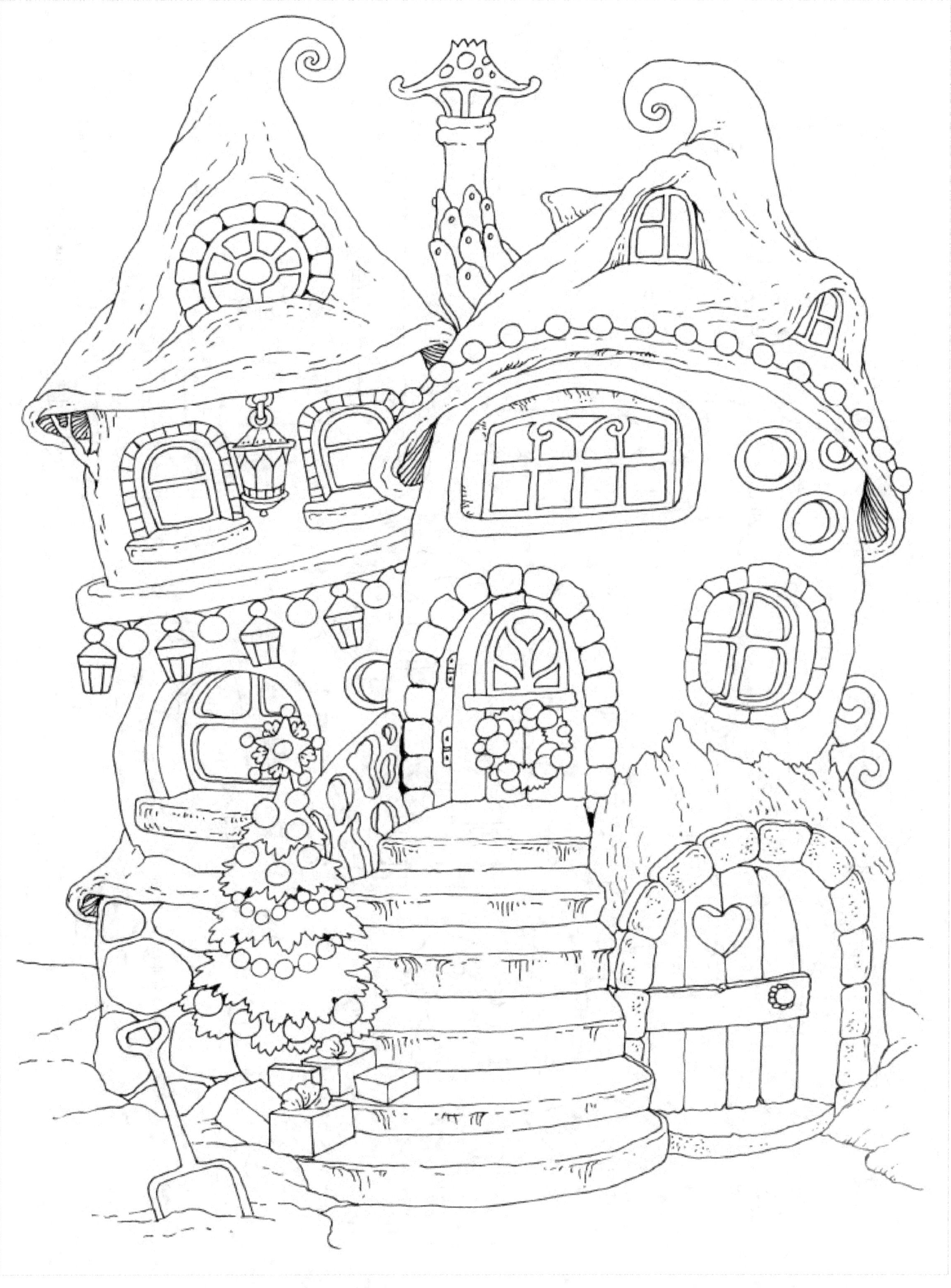

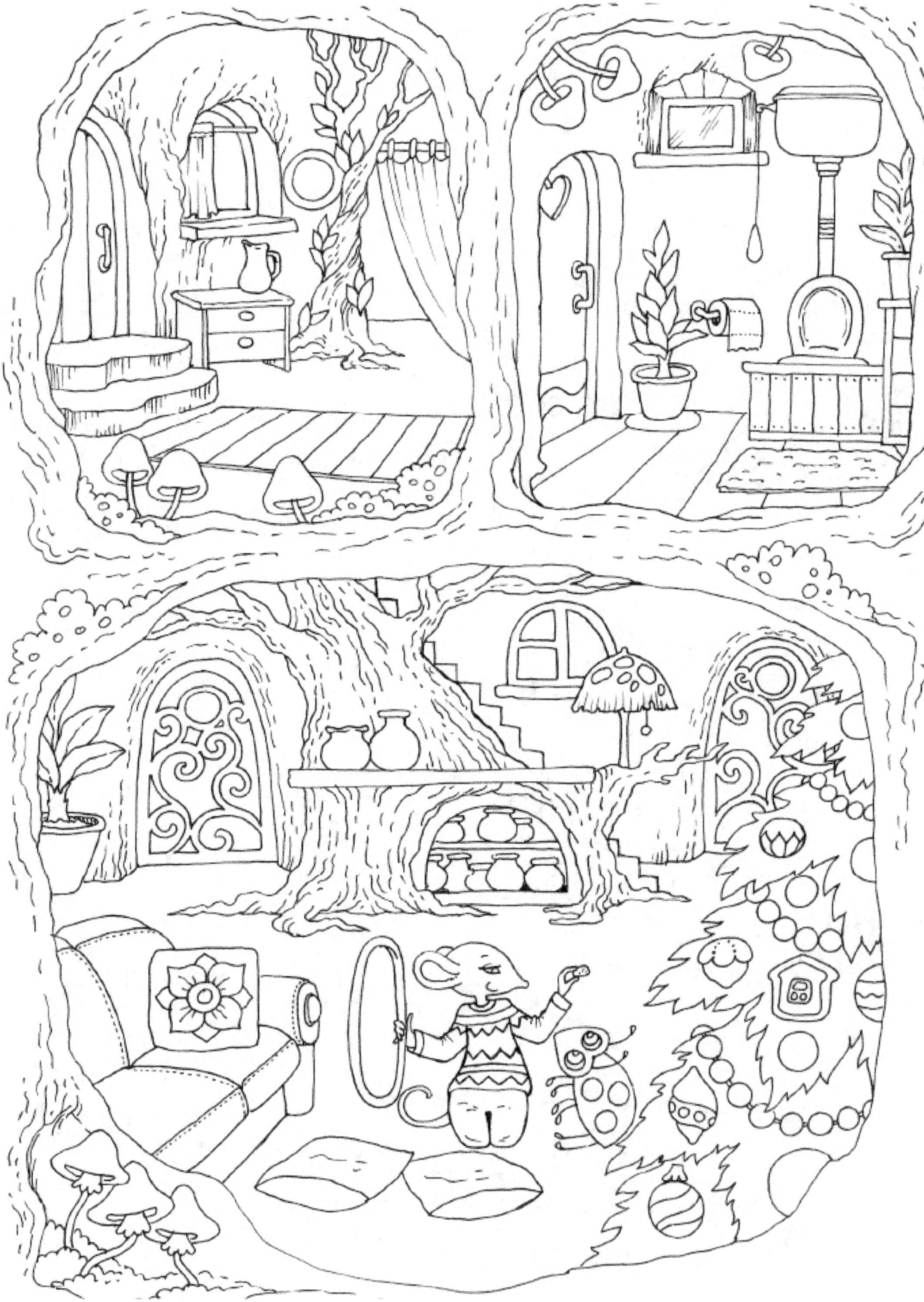

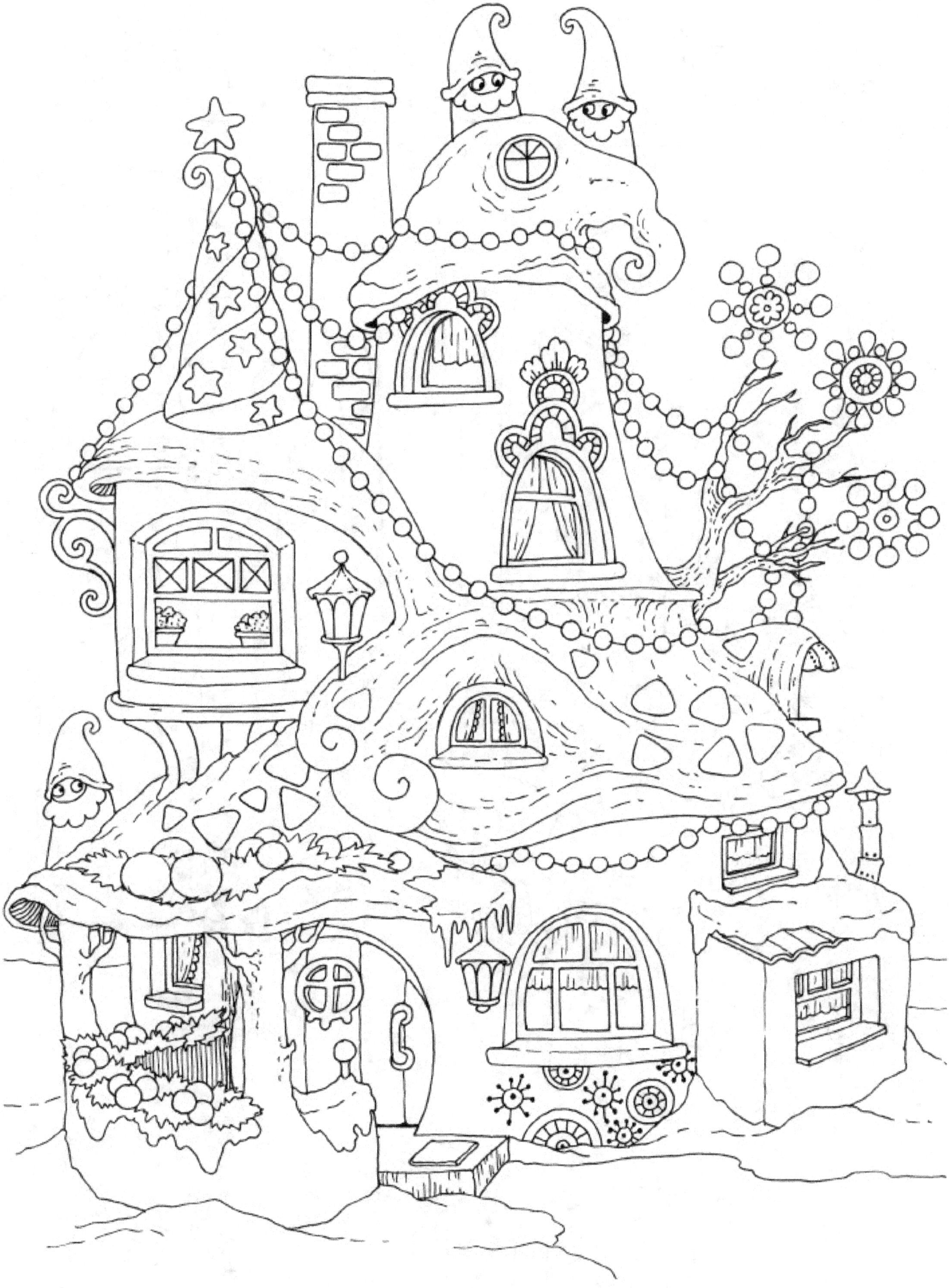

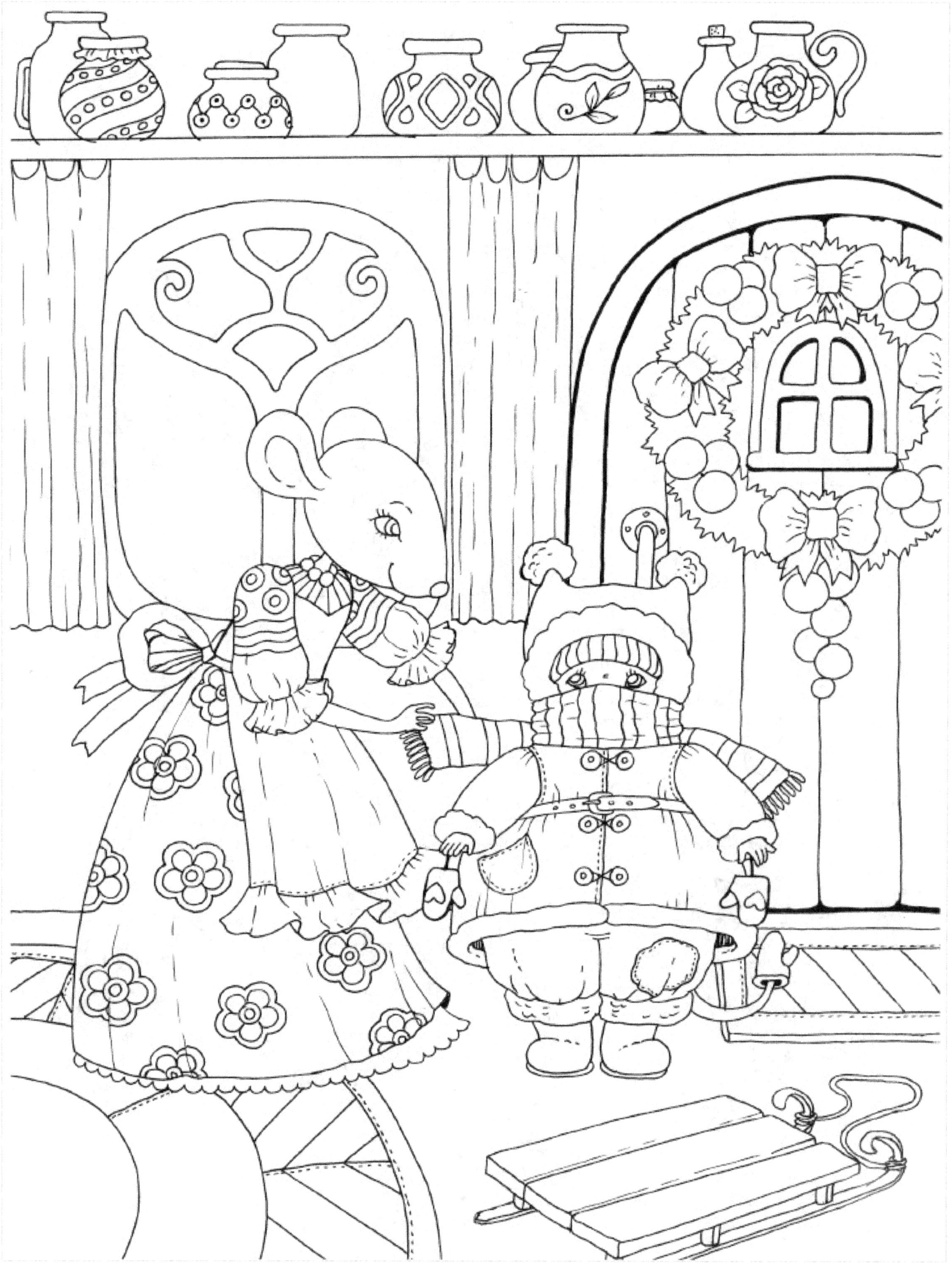

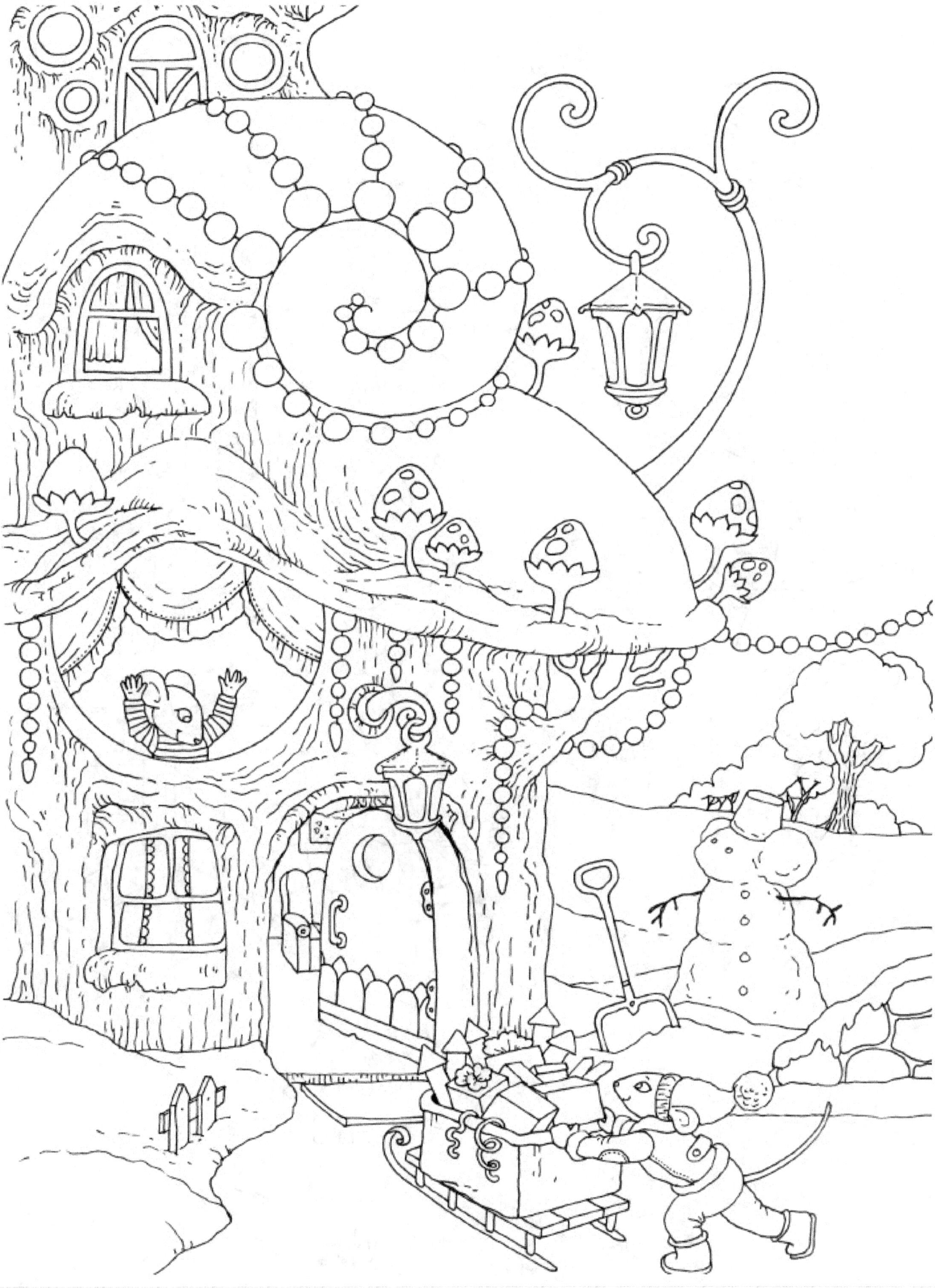

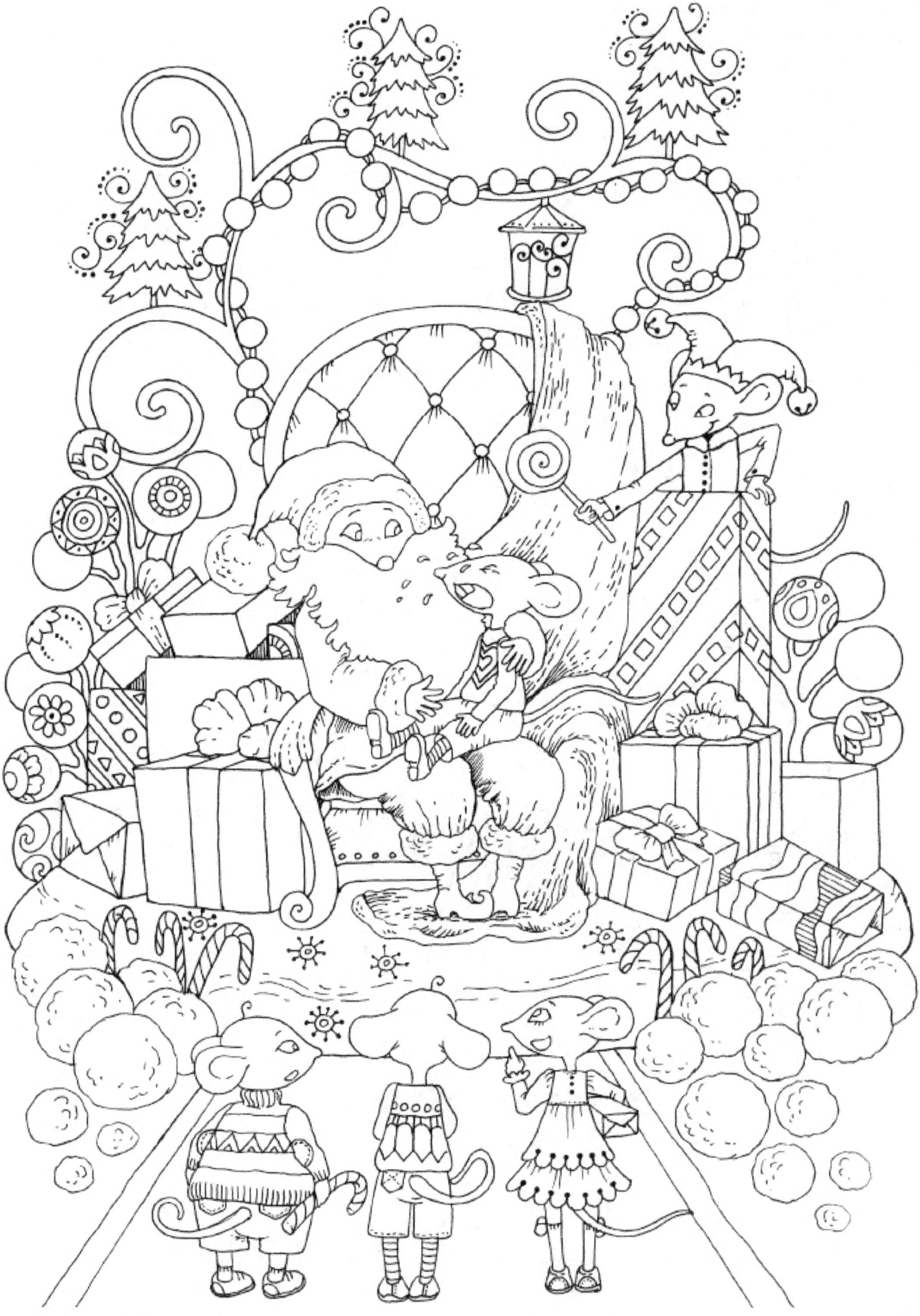

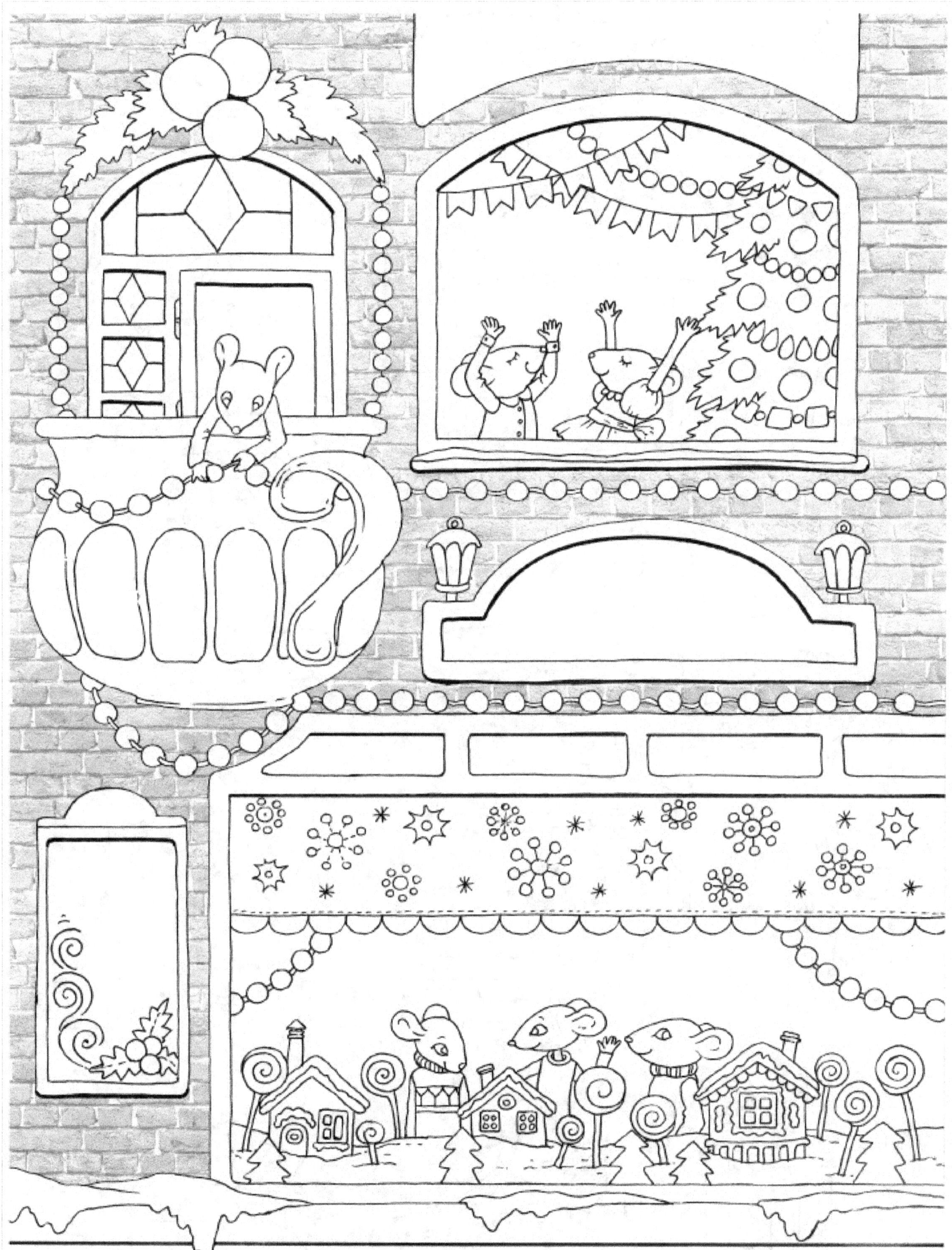

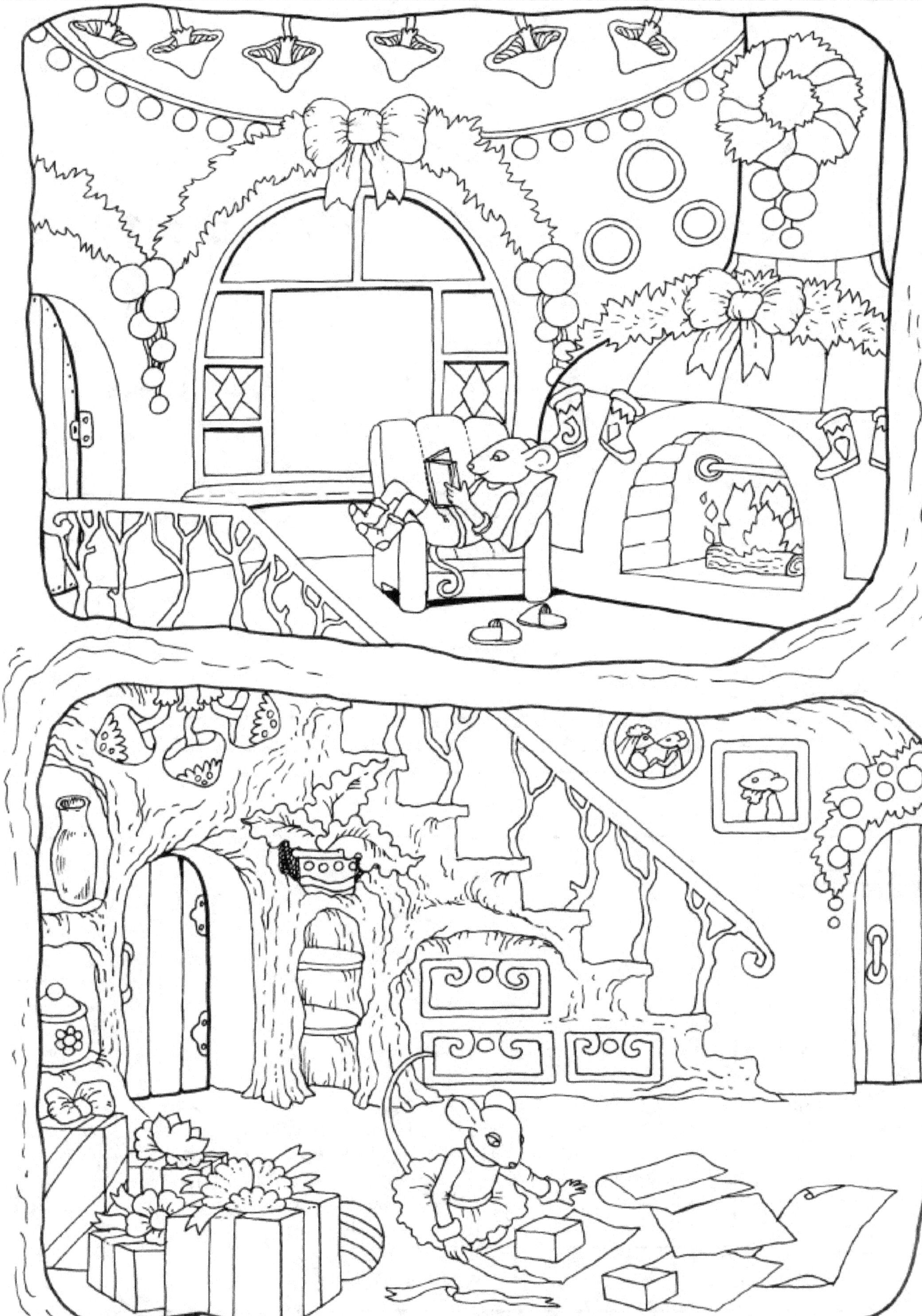

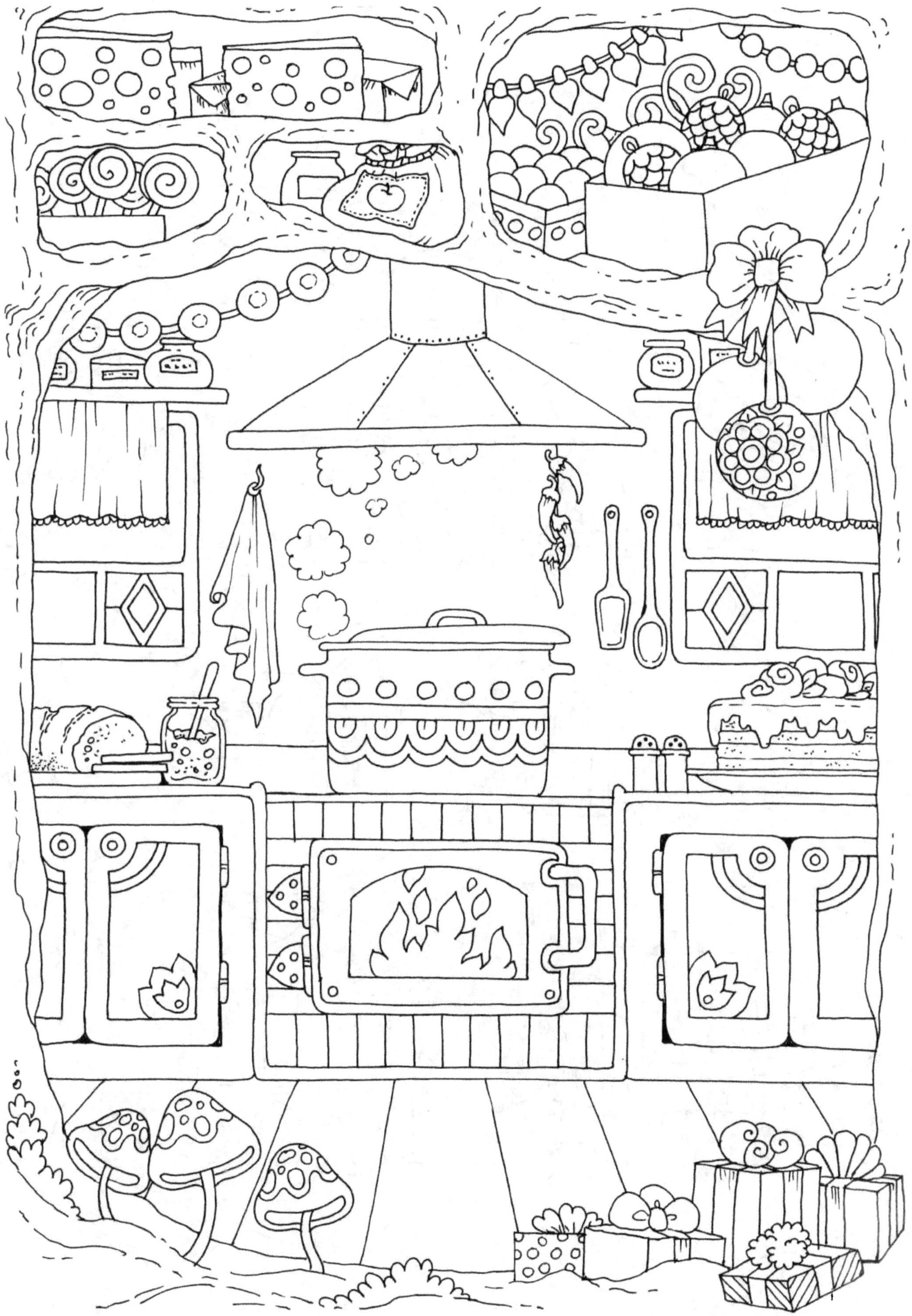

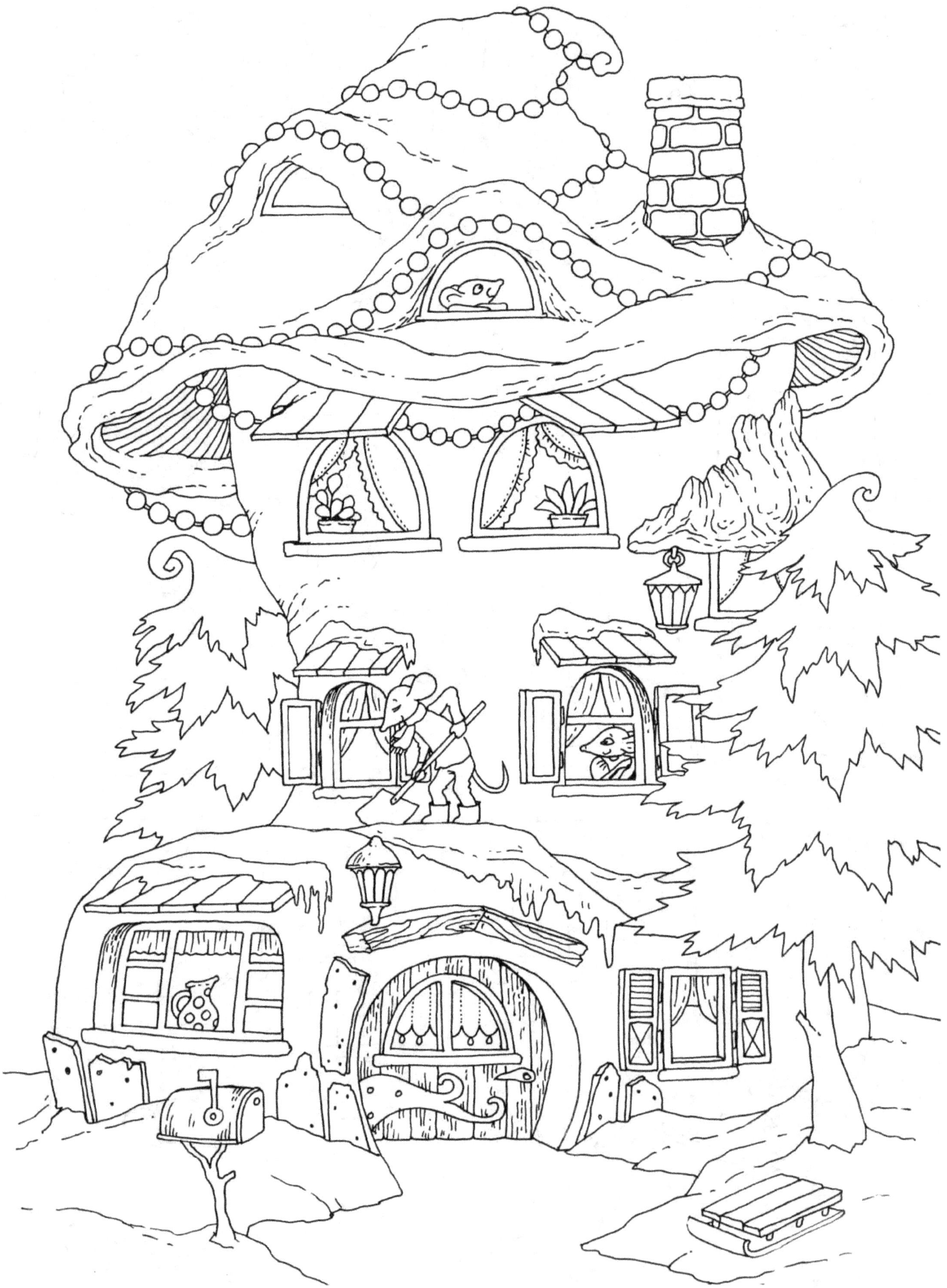

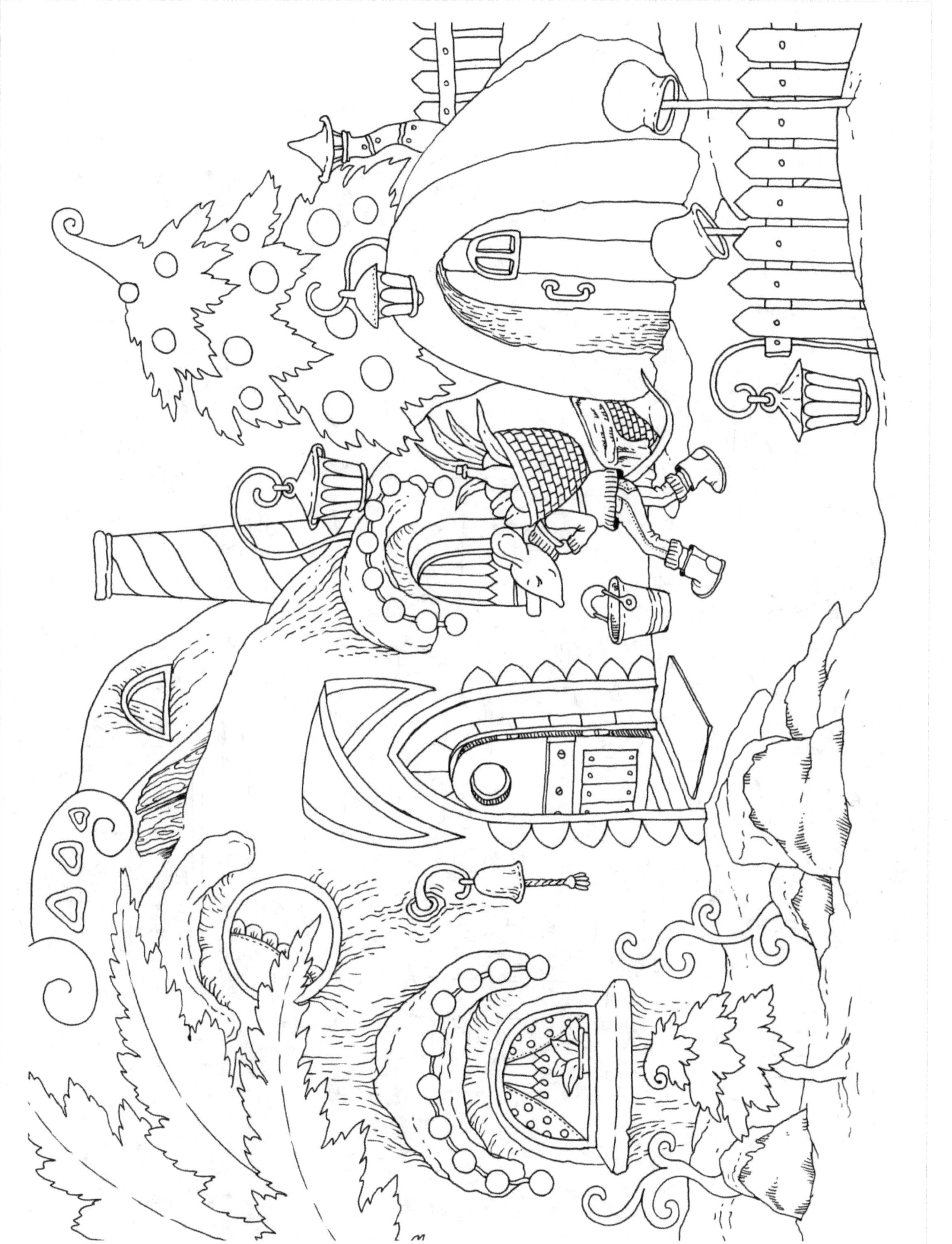

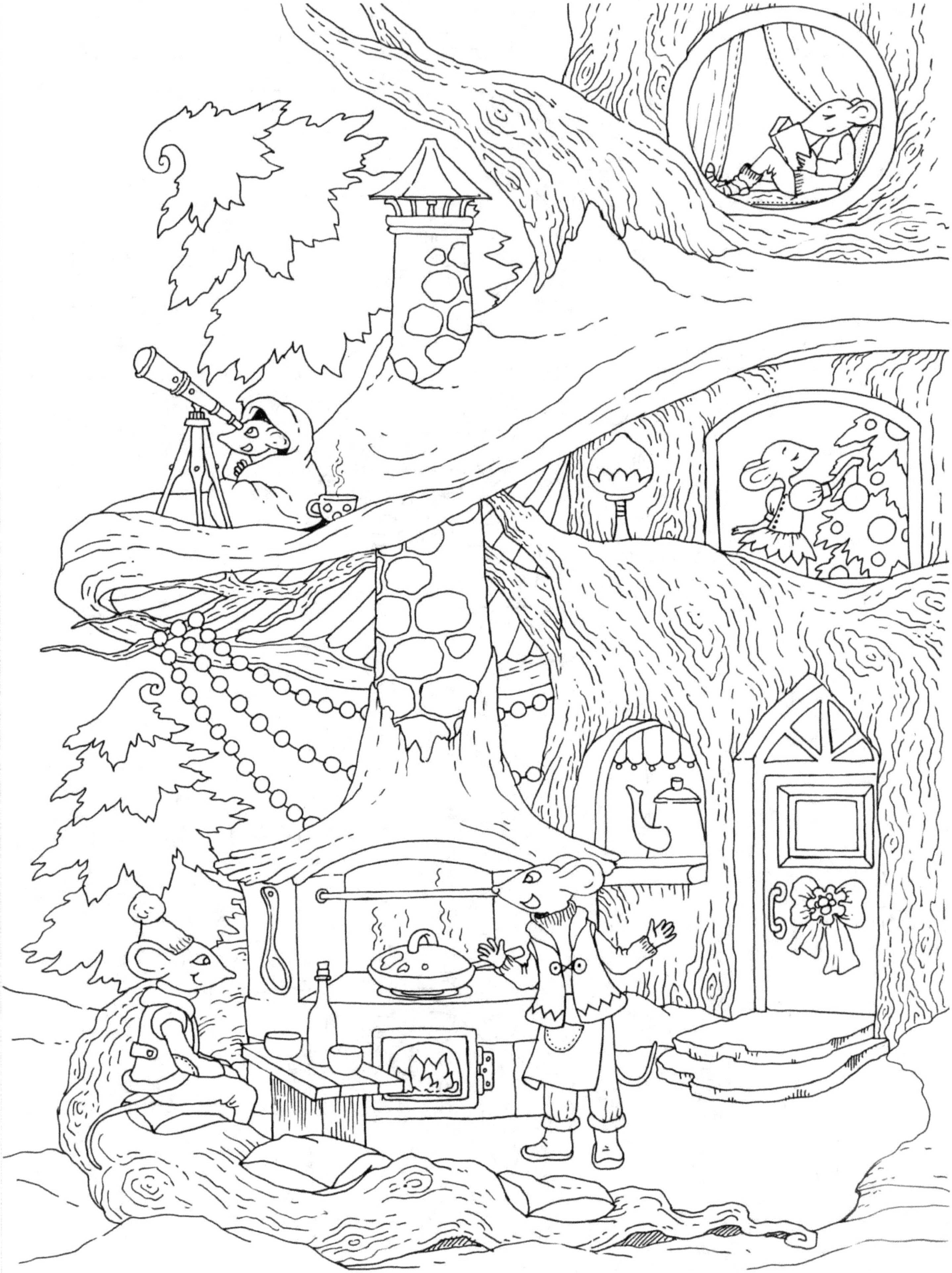

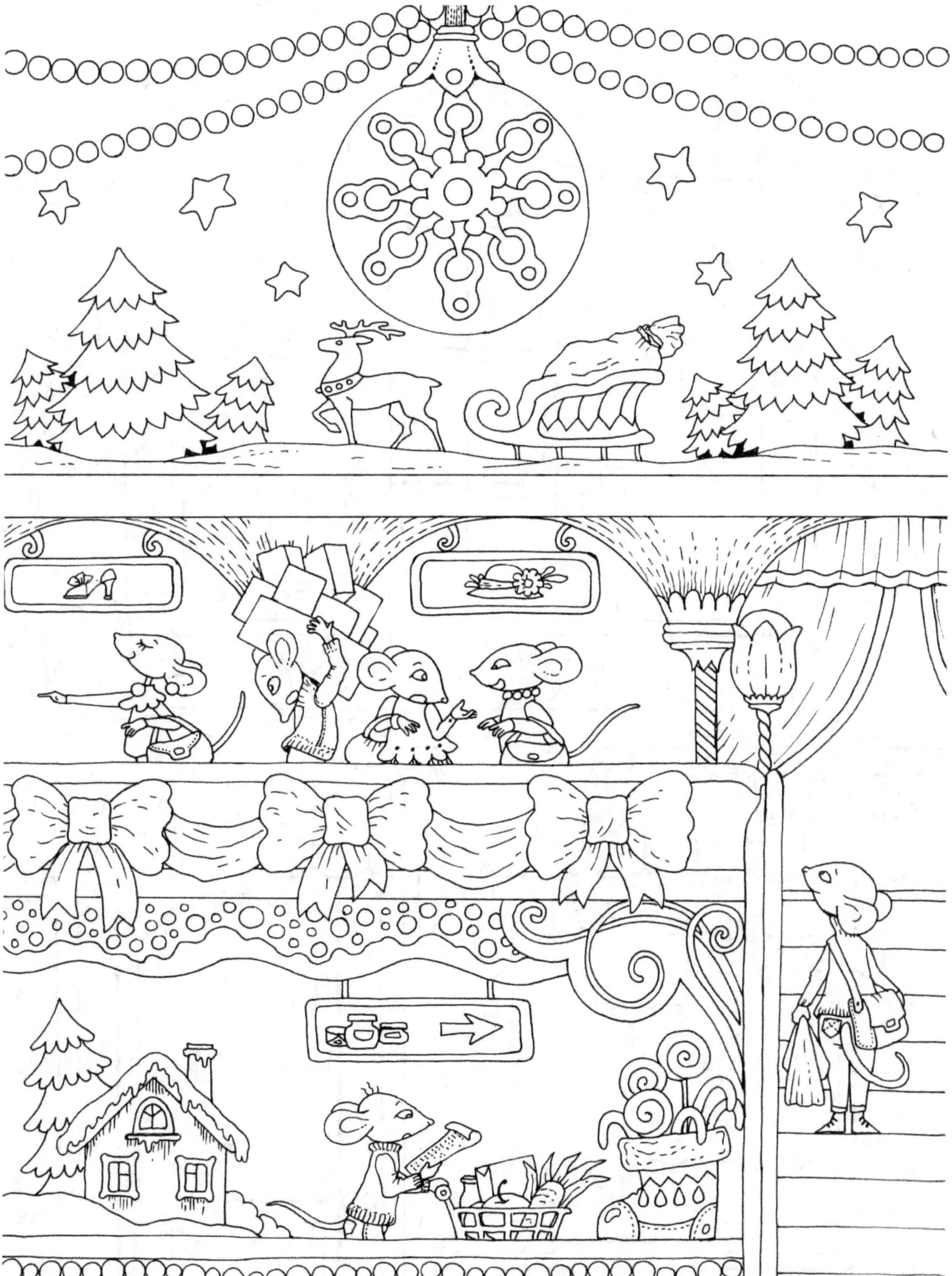

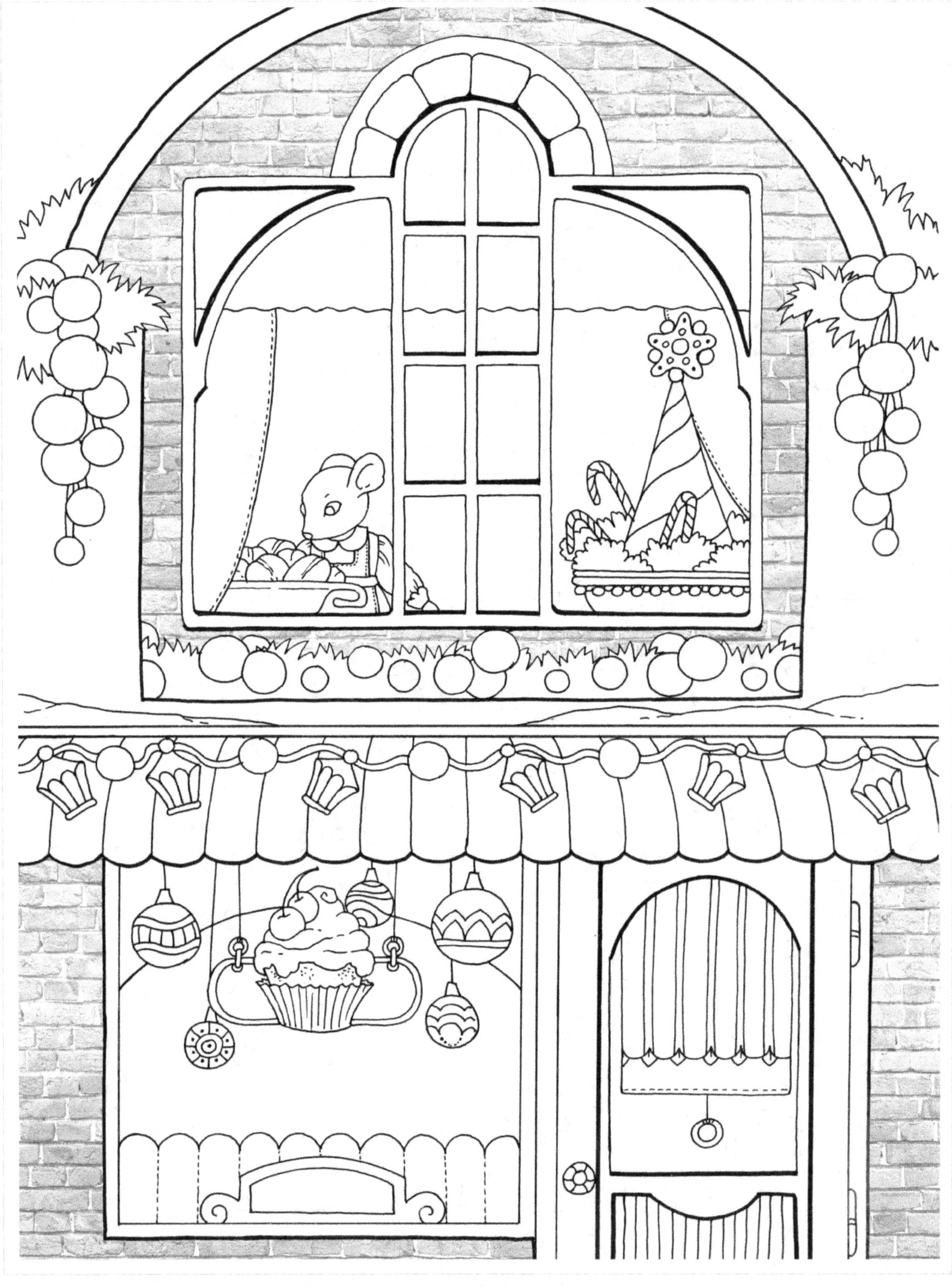

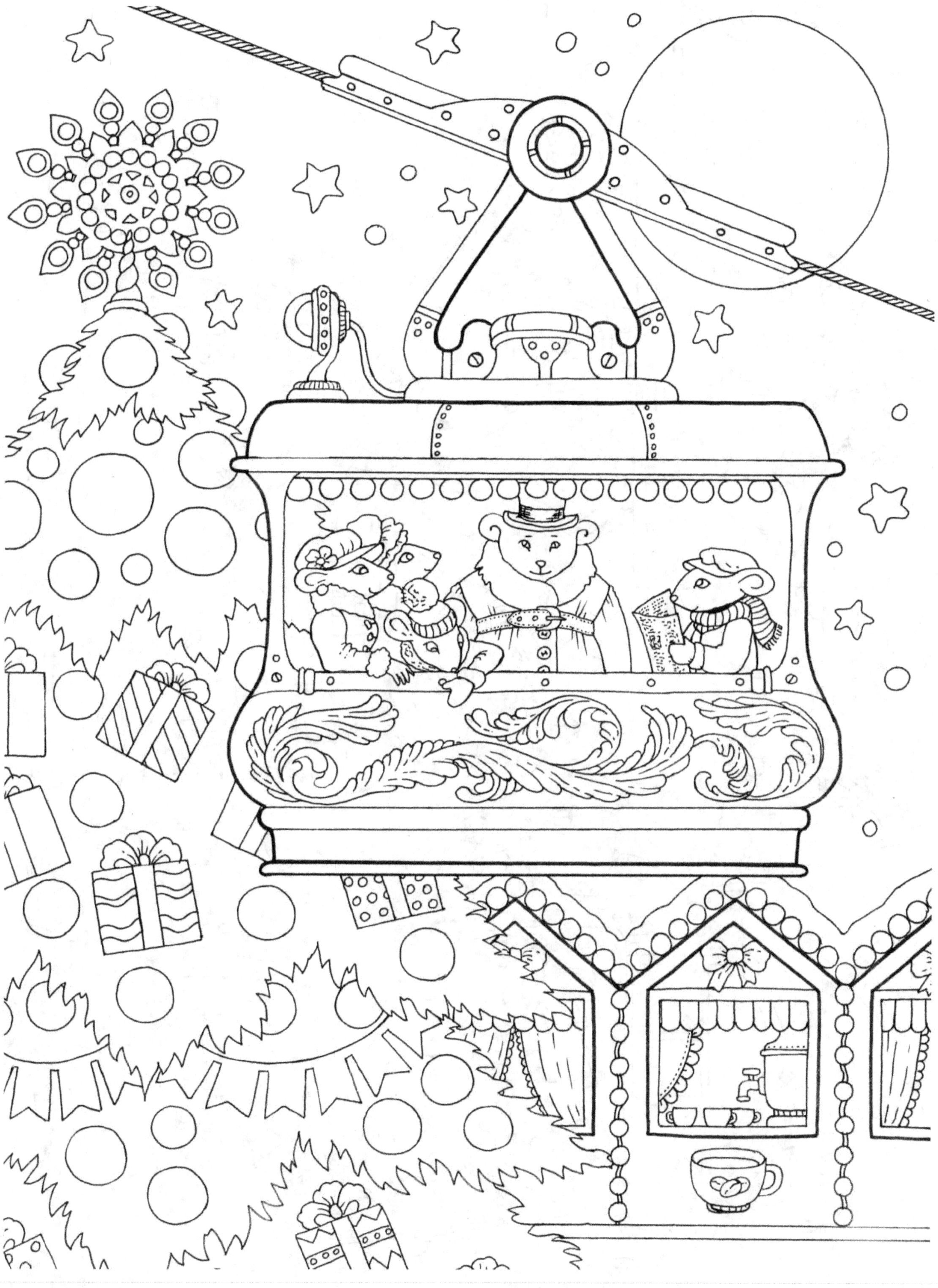

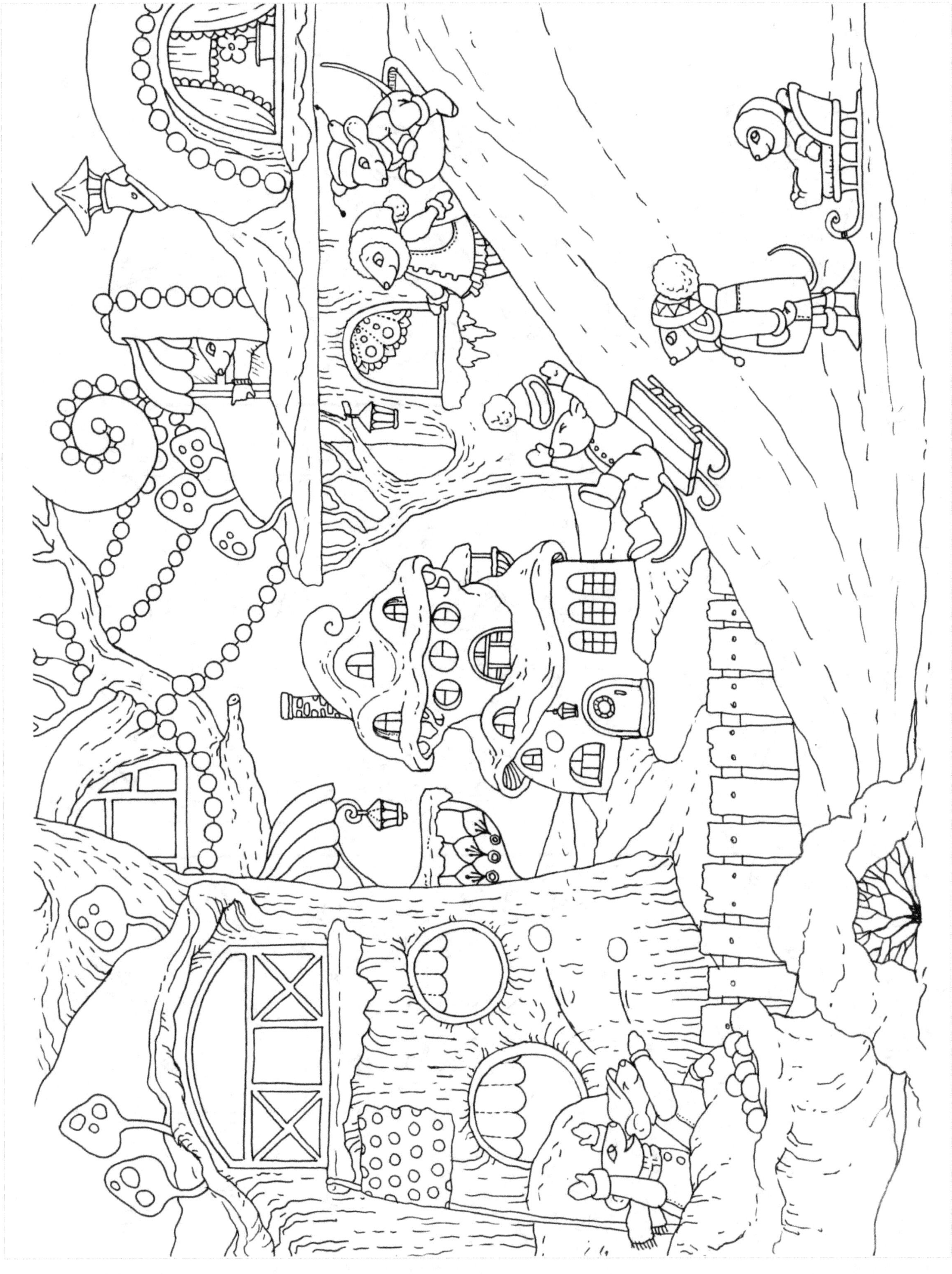

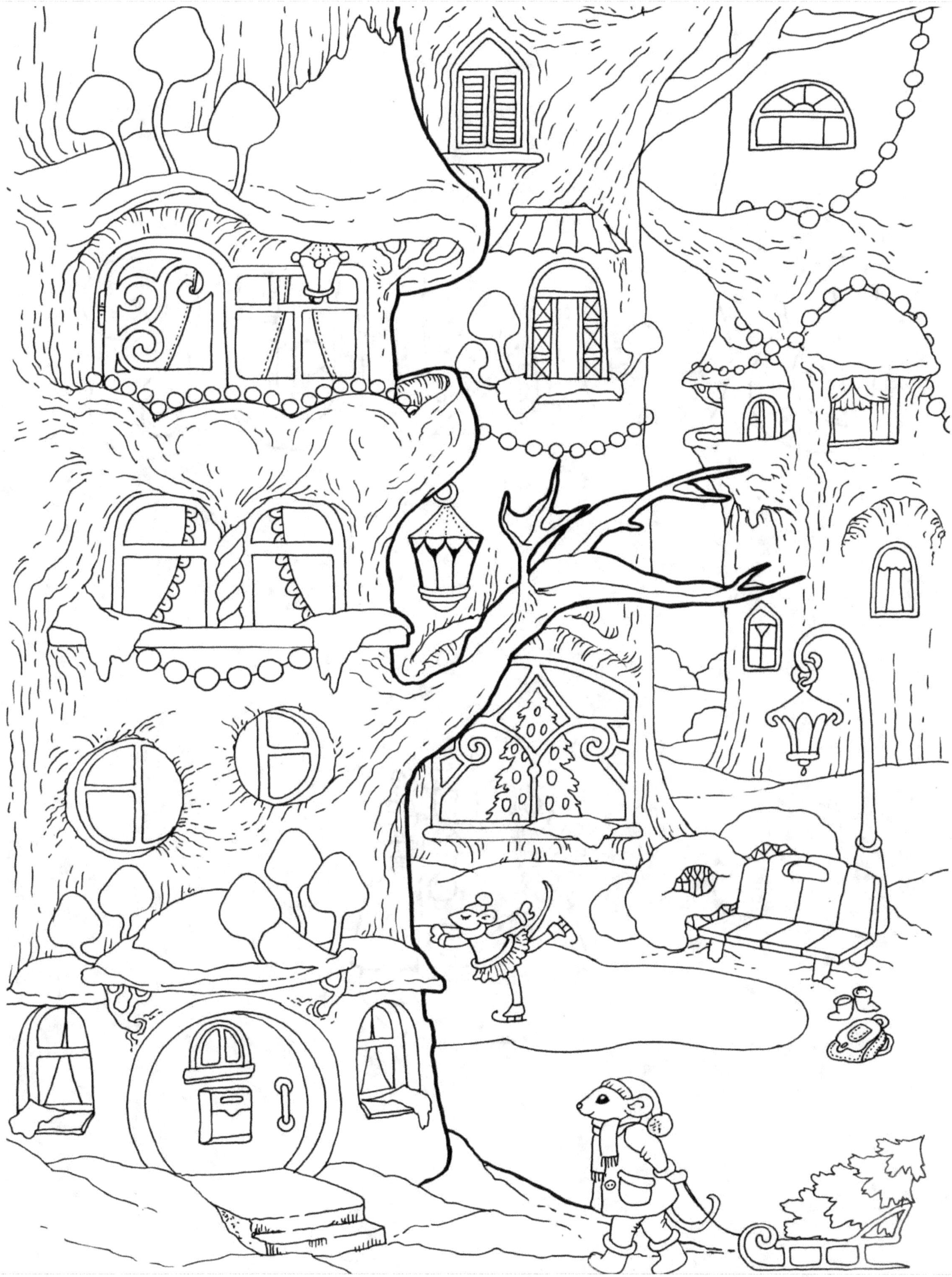

BONUS

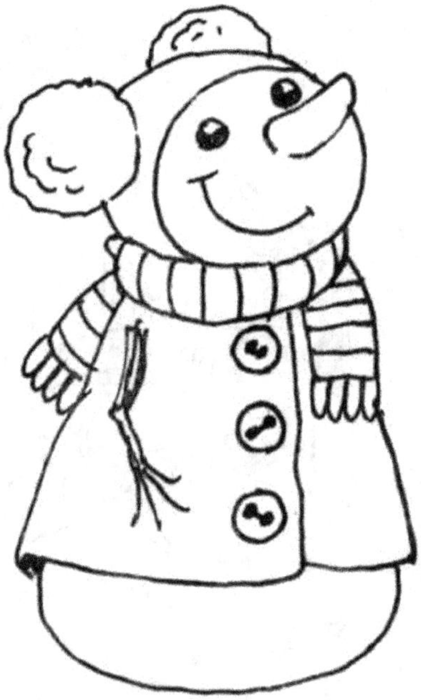

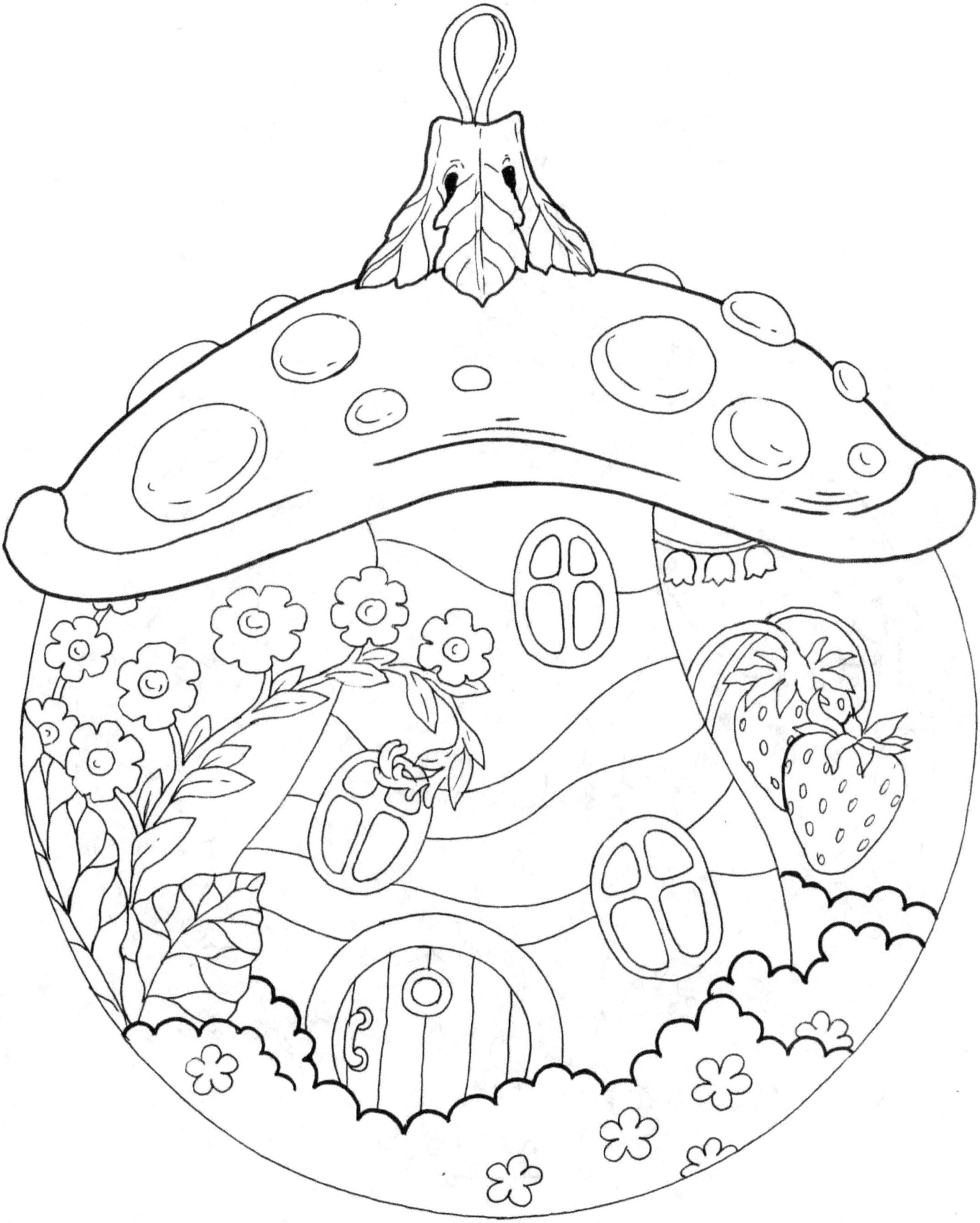

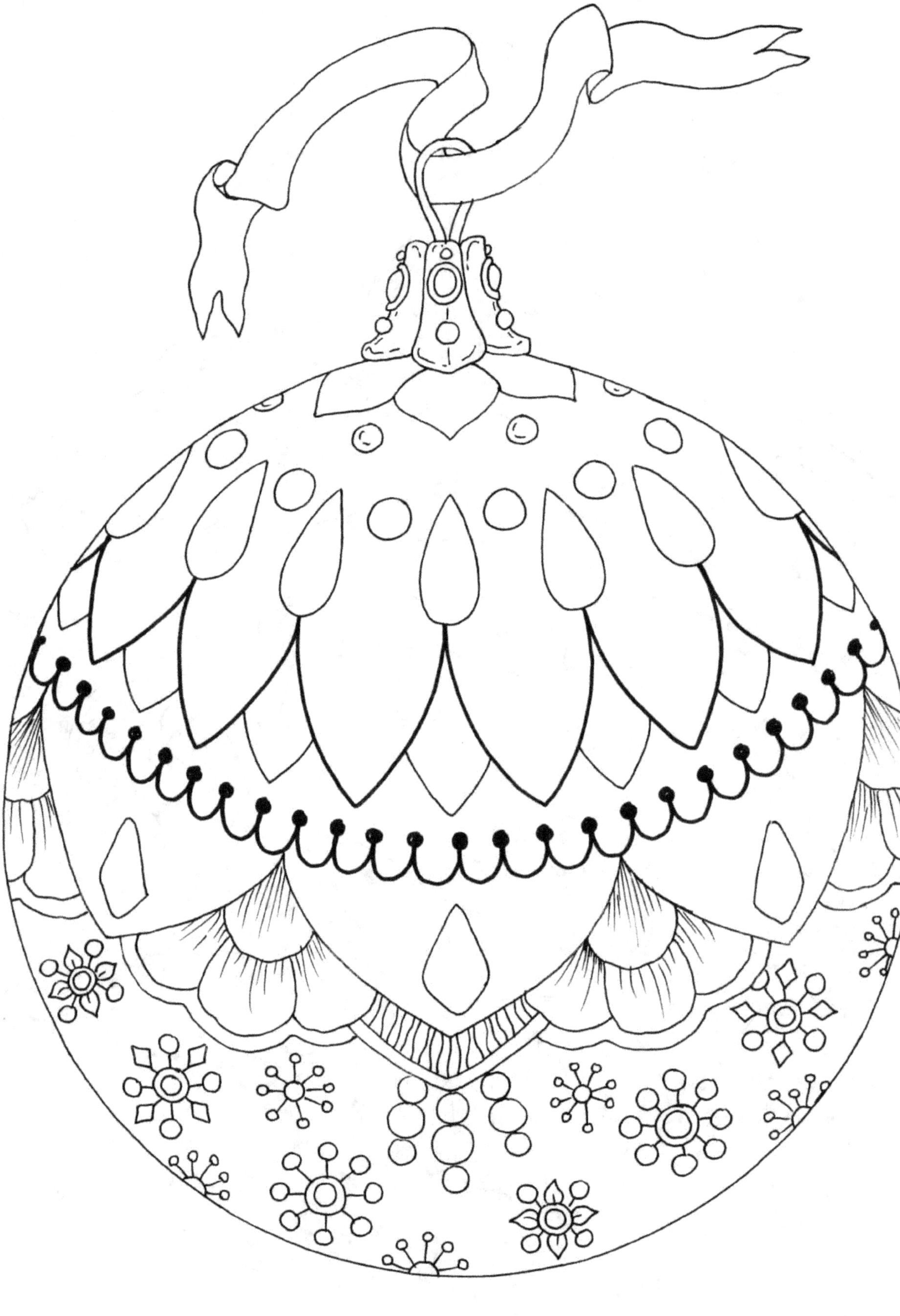

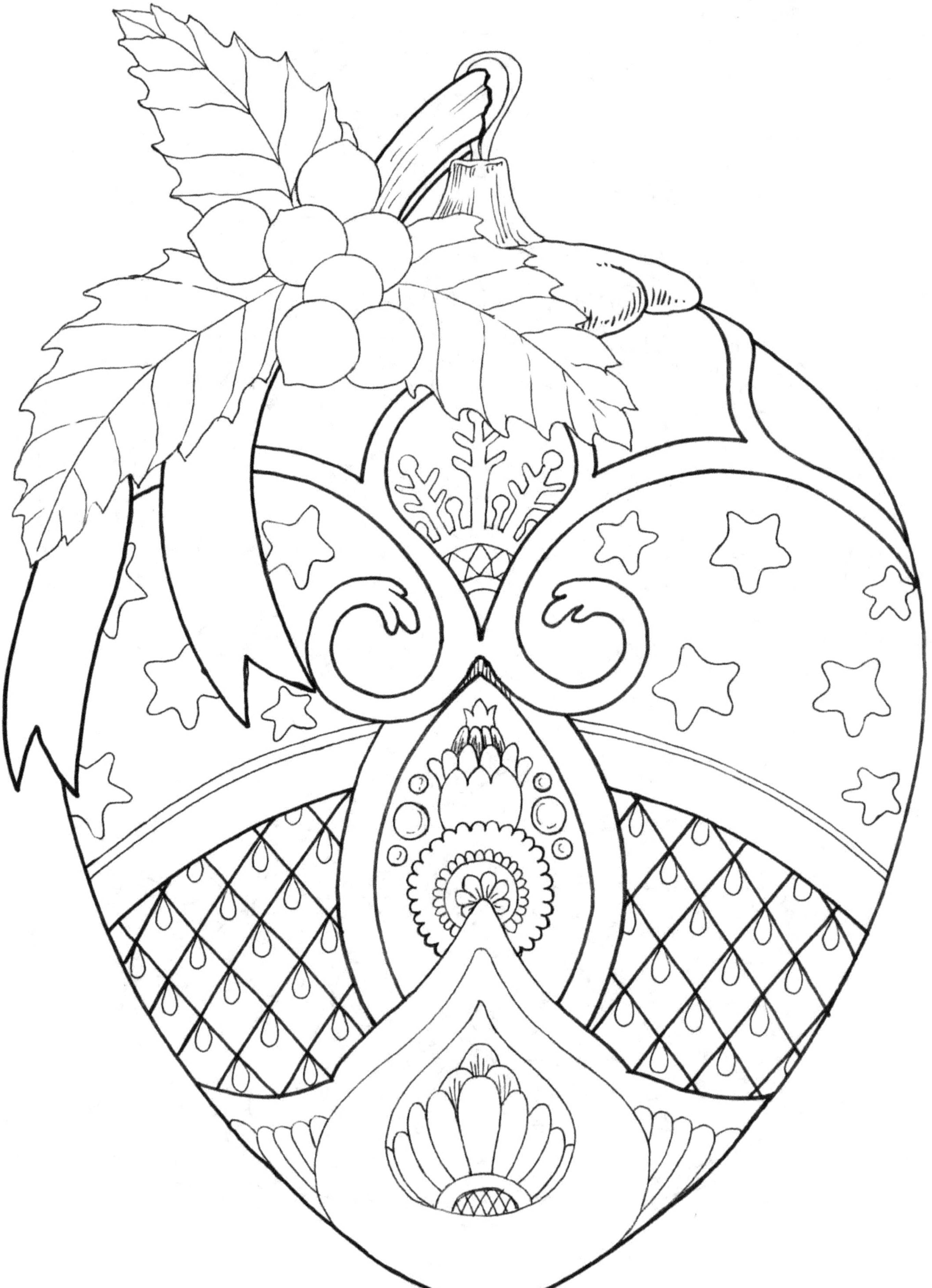

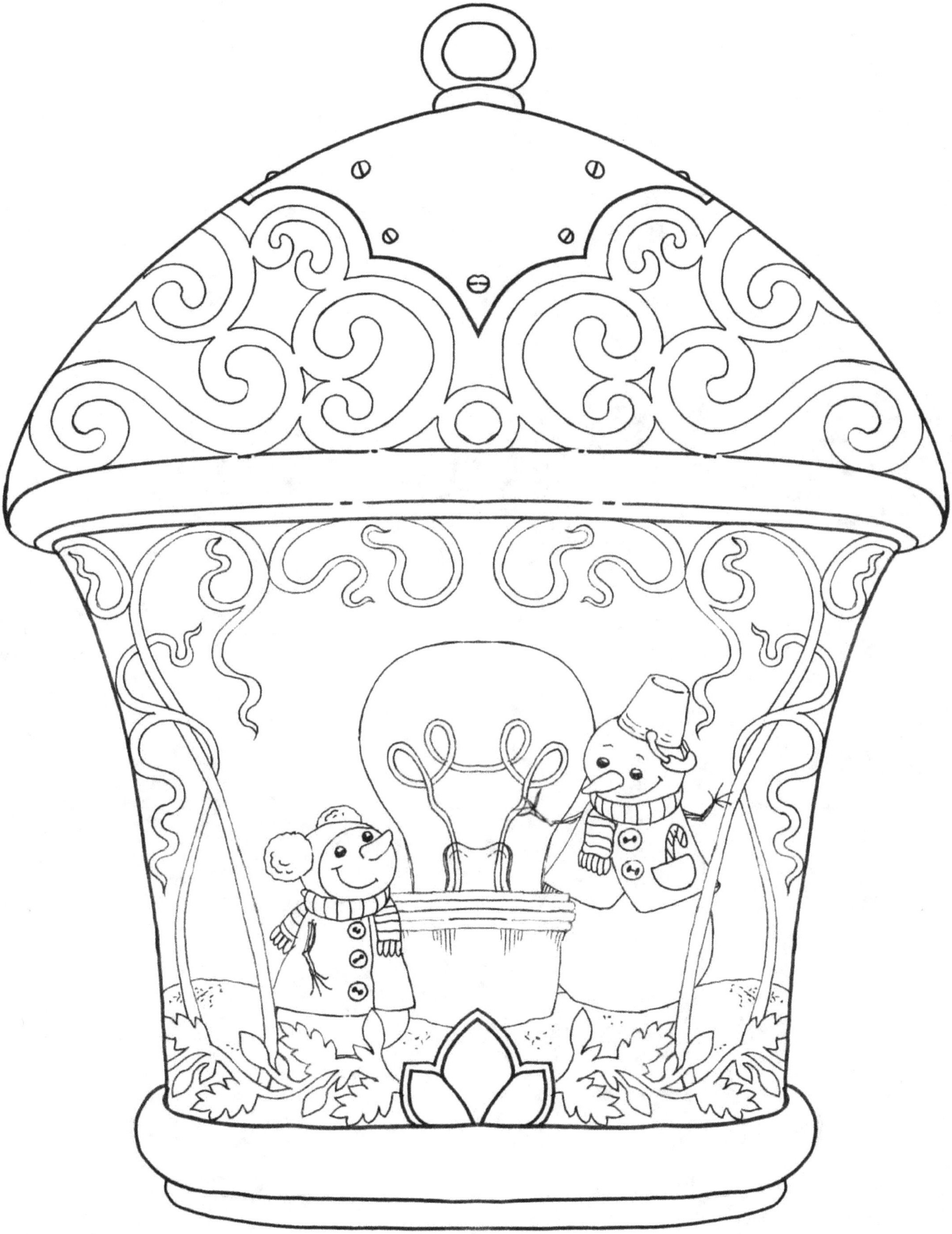

www.ingramcontent.com/pod-product-compliance
Lightning Source LLC
Chambersburg PA
CBHW081532220526
45467CB00010B/3142
* 9 7 9 8 7 3 0 1 0 2 6 5 1 *